WIN YOUR WAY INTO BIG MONEY HOLD'EM TOURNAMENTS

WIN YOUR WAY INTO BIG MONEY HOLD'EM TOURNAMENTS

HOW TO BEAT CASINO & ONLINE SATELLITE POKER TOURNAMENTS

Tom McEvoy
Brad Daugherty

CARDOZA PUBLISHING

Cardoza Publishing is the foremost gaming publisher in the world, with a library of over 100 up-to-date and easy-to-read books and strategies. These authoritative works are written by the top experts in their fields and, with more than 7,500,000 books in print, represent the best-selling and most popular gaming books anywhere.

FIRST CARDOZA EDITION

Copyright © 2003, 2005 by Tom McEvoy,
Brad Daugherty and Dana Smith

- All Rights Reserved -

Library of Congress Catalog Card No: 2004101424
ISBN: 1-58042-147-4

Visit our new web site (www.cardozapub.com)
or write us for a full list of books and computer strategies.

CARDOZA PUBLISHING
P.O. Box 1500, Cooper Station, New York, NY 10276
Phone (800)577-WINS
email: cardozapub@aol.com
www.cardozapub.com

ABOUT THE AUTHORS

World Series of Poker Champions **Tom McEvoy** and **Brad Daugherty** are among the greatest tournament poker players today. They have won millions of dollars playing tournaments against the very best in the world.

McEvoy, the 1983 World Champion of Poker, has won four World Series titles. He is the author of the acclaimed *Championship Tournament Poker*, "one of the most important poker books of all time" according to Gamblers Book Club in Las Vegas, and co-author of ten other titles including *Championship No-Limit & Pot-Limit Hold'em*, *Championship Stud*, *Championship Omaha*, *The Championship Table*, *Championship Hold'em* and *No-Limit Texas Hold'em*.

Daugherty, the 1991 World Champion of Poker, was the first player in World Series of Poker history to win $1 million. Two years after winning the title, he came close again, appearing at the championship table at the 1993 World Series of Poker. He has won countless tournaments and is one of the most feared poker players today in both on-land and online tournaments. He is also the co-author, with McEvoy, of *No-Limit Texas Hold'em*.

TABLE OF CONTENTS

Introduction

You hold in your hands the key to earning a shot at fame and fortune. In the following pages, we'll show you how to win your way into big money tournaments that have turned amateurs into multi-millionaires almost overnight. In the past six years alone, four amateurs—Noel Furlong (1999), Robert Varkonyi (2002), Chris Moneymaker (2003), and Greg Raymer (2004)—have parlayed nominal investments into winnings totaling more than $10 million and world championship titles. And lots of other players have won tens of thousands, hundreds of thousands and millions of dollars playing satellite tournaments. You might be next!

We've earned millions of dollars by mastering the art of satellite play, and now we're going to share our secrets with you. Even if you have never played a satellite before, have no fear. We'll explain where to find them, which ones to enter, how to play, and then how to beat these mini-tournaments.

Eleven major sections give you specific proven strategies for winning no-limit and limit hold'em satellites and earning entry into any tournament you want to play. Step-by-step, you'll learn proven insider strategies for beating limit and no-limit hold'em satellites, as well as on table, multi-table, online and super satellites. And since you'll use many of the same strategies to win satellites and tournaments, you will also improve your chances of winning the big events.

Both of us have been fortunate enough to win the World Championship of Poker, and we hope that this book will help you to join us in the winner's circle one day. Let's move on and see how you might take that first step.

Overview: Turning a Toothpick into a Lumberyard

The first satellite in history was a one-table satellite for the World Series of Poker at Binion's Horseshoe in Las Vegas in the late 1970s. Eric Drache, the tournament director of the WSOP in the early days, was continually encouraging players to sign up for the $10,000 championship event because he always wanted to top the previous year's figures by at least one player. Drache had been having trouble getting people to enter the tournament when he noticed a pot-limit hold'em cash game with $5-$10 blinds going strong.

All of the players at the table, mostly Texas road gamblers, had about $1,000 each, making around $10,000 total on the table—the cost of a buy-in for the championship event. "Why don't you gentlemen put up $1,000 apiece and play a freezeout for a seat in the Big One?" he suggested. They did, and the first tournament satellite was born.

About five or six years later in 1983, Tom McEvoy won a seat in the championship event at the WSOP by winning a one-table satellite at Binion's Horseshoe, only a few days after he had won the limit hold'em title at the WSOP. He went on to make history by becoming the first satellite winner to go on to win the championship bracelet. That same year, the Bingo Palace (now called Palace Station) held four $100 buy-in, no-rebuy "super" satellites for the WSOP championship event. Each winner-take-all satellite was limited to 100 players. Two of the four Bingo Palace satellite winners made it to the championship table—Rod Peate finished second to McEvoy, and Robbie Geers finished fifth. Geers also finished in the money twenty years later at the 2003 WSOP main event.

Nowadays, of course, more than one-half of the players in the main event earn their entry fees via a satellite win. Many of them have gone on to win the Big One—Noel Furlong in 1999, Robert Varkonyi in 2002, Chris Moneymaker in 2003, and Greg Raymer in 2004, to name a few.

As satellites have become increasingly popular among players, so has their level of competence. Players are studying poker books, discussing with friends what works and what doesn't, and practicing on the Internet. Playing Internet satellites is particularly valuable because players can access hand histories, which can assist them in getting a line on how their opponents play, as well as allow them to study their own statistics. For example, you can download the last 150 hands that you played. Using this information, you can determine which types of hands you have won with and which you have lost with. And you can get a full account of what has gone on in the pots that you've played, which will help you determine whether you've been playing too many hands or too few, too loose or too tight.

Thanks to satellites, you now have a chance to enter the main tournament for about 10 percent of the tournament buy-in rather than having to reach into your pocket for the full entry fee. For example, on the day before or early in the morning of a big tournament, a lot of players who cannot afford a $1,000 tournament buy-in, but who can round up $115 to $125, are waiting in line to play a satellite for that day's event.

Even players with big bankrolls like to get into tournaments cheaply. Players who can afford the $1,000 buy-in may want to practice a game they haven't played for a while, and they always like the opportunity to save money through a satellite win. As soon as ten people have posted their satellite buy-ins, they play a winner-take-all mini-tournament with the winner gaining a seat in the main tournament. As a result, tournament fields have increased tremendously.

In fact the growth of the championship event at the World Series of Poker is directly related to the growth of satellites. When Tom McEvoy won the World Championship in 1983 and went down in WSOP history as the first satellite winner to win the Big One, there were 108 entrants in the championship event. Eight years later in 1991 when Brad Daugherty won the World Championship and went down in history as the first champion to receive $1 million, the field had increased to 215 players. By 2003 when Chris Moneymaker won a record $2.5 million and became the first online satellite winner to become World Champion of Poker, the field had mushroomed to 839. In fact more than half of the entrants in the 2003 WSOP $10,000 buy-in championship event won their seats via a satellite.

In 2004 Greg Raymer won a seat at the Big One by winning a $150 buy-in double shootout on PokerStars. When he went on to win the bracelet, he became the second consecutive PokerStars player to win the championship. David Williams, who was the runner-up to Raymer, and Mike McClain and Matt Dean, who both made the final table, also won their way into the WSOP through satellites at PokerStars. Like Raymer, Williams won a double shootout, while McClain won a $615 satellite, and Dean won a $30 re-buy tournament, in which he made only one add-on. Josh Ariah, who finished third, is a regular player on PokerStars.

Satellites for the Big One have become an international phenomenon. Satellite players win their seats in online casino satellites, on-land casinos, big casinos, hometown casinos,

American Indian casinos, and European casinos. Binion's Horseshoe in Las Vegas starts a two-tier satellite program every January in which you have to win a $125 one-table satellite in order to advance to the second tier, where ten first tier winners play off for a $10,000 seat in the Big One. Second place receives $300, and third place receives $200. These two-tier satellites are run until halfway through the WSOP. During the 2003 WSOP, the Horseshoe also offered super satellites with multiple rebuys two times every day. The final two super satellites held the day before the Big One started awarded a total of twenty-eight seats, which set a new record for the number of seats won in super satellites in one day.

Some Fantastic Satellite Parlays

Internet satellite winners Chris Moneymaker and Greg Raymer have made two of the greatest parlays of all time when they turned small investments into huge winnings. Moneymaker parlayed $39 into $2.5 million in 2003, and Raymer turned $150 into $5 million in 2004, but they aren't the only tournament players who have parlayed small investments into big wins. Back when satellites were still in their infancy, Rod Peate paid $110 to enter a 100-player no-rebuy satellite, which he won. Peate parlayed that win into $216,000 by finishing second to McEvoy at the 1983 WSOP main event.

That same year, Hans "Tuna" Lund won a $1,000 one-table satellite at Caesar's Lake Tahoe for a $10,000 buy-in to Amarillo Slim's Super Bowl of Poker. Lund outlasted 1982 World Champion of Poker Jack Straus in heads-up play at the championship table, winning the tournament, $180,000, and a big diamond ring.

Journalist and author Jim McManus made a parlay of a different sort. Using the $4,000 advance that he received from Harper's magazine to write an article about the 2000 WSOP and the Ted Binion murder case, he won a $1,030 satellite seat for the Big One. He finished fifth to champion Chris Ferguson and runner-up T.J. Cloutier for a win of $247,760. Three years later he parlayed his adventures in Las Vegas into a book contract with Harper Row Publishing. *Positively Fifth Street* was named one of the top five non-instructional poker books of all time by the *Las Vegas Sun* newspaper and made Amazon's Best Seller list. McManus recently sold the movie rights to the book.

The Upside of Playing Satellites

The biggest upside of playing satellites is that you can win a seat in the tournament for a fraction of the cost of the tournament buy-in. Saving money is, in fact, the primary purpose of playing satellites. Sometimes that is your only way of getting into an event. The tournament buy-in may be beyond your bankroll, but the satellite isn't, so you should give yourself one or two satellite shots at getting into the event you want to play. If you win one, you're in the tournament for a reduced price, and if you lose a satellite or two, you have lost only a limited investment. Satellites also help to build large fields for tournaments, which leads to increased prize pools, meaning you have a chance at winning more money.

Playing satellites allows you to practice a game that you haven't played in a while and feel rusty at. Let's say that I don't normally play seven-card stud, but I think that I might want to play the tournament. So I go play a seven-card stud satellite, and it helps me get back my "feel" for the game and determine whether I still have enough ability at it to be competitive. Playing a satellite also lets you practice playing your favorite cash game in tournament mode. It's a good way to warm up for the main event.

You also can practice playing a new game that

you aren't familiar with. At the 2003 WSOP, for example, there were several players who wanted to play the triple draw lowball event but had never played the game before. Triple draw lowball is not regularly spread in casino cash games except at very high stakes, so unless you want to play $200/$400 or $300/$600, how are you going to practice the game? Players new to the game said, "I'll go play a satellite or two for it and learn how to play the game. Then if I win a satellite, I'll play the tournament." You can do the same thing for other rarely spread high-stakes games such as deuce-to-seven draw, a traditional Southern poker game that is popular among high-stakes players. You may not be able to sit down in a cash game, but almost anyone can afford to play a satellite.

Another advantage of playing satellites is that you can learn the skills of shorthanded play or practice your existing shorthanded skills. Every time a player is eliminated from a ten-handed one-table satellite, you have to adjust your play, because a satellite is really a mini-tournament. It's a one-table situation, but you're starting at the final table. If you have hopes of winning a multi-table satellite (such as those held at the Horseshoe, Foxwoods, Bellagio and Commerce casinos), you have to learn to play ten-handed, nine-handed, eight-handed, and so on down the line until you eventually get heads-up with somebody. One-table satellites are good places to learn how to compete in shorthanded situations. Playing satellites also can help you to hone your skills for final-table play in tournaments. Almost all successful tournament players also are great satellite players.

Getting to play against some of the top players is a feature of satellites that appeals to a lot of players. Sitting down at a one-table satellite with players you've never faced before, famous or unknown, gives you a chance to watch their play and practice reading them. You can find out how aggressive they are, the types of bad plays they are prone to make, the successful moves they make, and so on. Getting a feel for players that you don't know can be an advantage to you when you play with them later in any event.

At the major tournaments, a lot of players sign up to play one-table satellites with celebrity players, because they might never get the opportunity to play against them in a side game or even in a tournament. Even the more famous players try to save money by playing satellites. And occasionally you'll see players in the high-limit games, $5,000-$10,000 and up, that you wouldn't be able to sit down and play with because of bankroll restrictions. But on the morning of the tournament, these high-stakes players will sometimes wander over and play a satellite, giving you a chance to sit down and play with them. Playing satellites with celebs, world champions, and high-stakes players can be both educational and fun. It also can give you certain bragging rights: "Guess who I knocked out of the satellite? Tom McEvoy! I'm just a $4/$8 player and I sent a world champion to the rail!"

For good players, satellites certainly can be a profitable deal. And even weaker players with a limited budget get a shot at a cheap tournament seat. McEvoy admits that he owes a lot of his poker success to winning a satellite seat in the championship event in '83. As a consequence, he is a big believer in the satellite system for all sizes of bankrolls. Satellites offer good practice and make sound economic sense for the shorter bankrolls. The bigger bankrolls probably are going to play anyway, and so they may not want to waste their time playing satellites when they could be playing bigger action cash games. Other top tournament players don't play satellites because they have a backer or a very big bankroll. Unfortunately most of us are not in either of these categories, so we have to go "economy fare" and take the satellite route.

The Downside of Playing Satellites

One disadvantage of playing satellites the morning of the tournament is that you can wear yourself out. And if you play too many satellites, you can get burned out to the point that you don't feel like playing the tournament. You can also wind up spending too much money playing satellites when you'd be better off just buying into the tournament in the first place. Satellites are especially useful when you know that you aren't going to buy into the tournament unless you win a satellite for it. But if you're going to play the tournament whether or not you win a seat for it, you should definitely limit your satellite play to conserve energy and finances. As in all aspects of poker, it is very important to manage your satellite money wisely.

The biggest downside of playing satellites is that most players don't understand proper satellite strategy. They play the "SOP" method of satellite strategy, by the Seat of their Pants. They get into their action mode and do whatever they think is appropriate at the moment, with no preconceived idea of what proper satellite strategy is. SOP satellite players are definitely at a disadvantage against those who use proper satellite strategy.

Win Your Way Into Big Money Hold'em Tournaments

You need to understand the basic concepts of how to play a particular type of satellite before you enter it so that you won't be burdened by the handicaps that unknowledgeable players have. Our goal in this book is to teach you how to get the edge over your opponents so that you always have the skill advantage. And we'll do this by setting forth the winning principles of satellite play and teaching you the special set of skills that will take you to the championship table via a satellite win.

Ten Ways to Win a Seat for the World Series

1

Satellites come in all shapes and sizes with a wide variety of formats and buy-ins. Some have one-table with ten players, others have two tables, and super satellites have multiple tables with as many 200 to 300 players. Not all satellites are for big buy-in tournaments — you can play a satellite for a $50 buy-in tournament, a $500 tournament, or a $5,000 tournament. You can even play a satellite to win a seat in the $25,000 buy-in championship event of the World Poker Tour.

If you want to play in the championship event at the World Series of Poker, you can win a seat for it in one or more of the following types of satellites. We explain the structure and setup of each type of satellite in more detail in Part Two.

1. Win a Satellite at an On-Land Casino

Casinos around the world begin offering WSOP satellites early in the year. Foxwoods in Connecticut, Hustler Casino in Southern California, Lucky Chances and Bay 101 in Northern California, and the Aviation Club in Paris, France, are just a few. Most of these satellites are for a seat in the championship event only, but casinos occasionally offer satellites for other WSOP events as well.

2. Win an Online Satellite

You can win your way into a World Series of Poker event by winning an online satellite. In 2003 Pokerstars.com set a new record by sending thirty-seven players to the championship event—two of whom cashed—the most players ever to win a WSOP seat through a venue other than the Horseshoe itself. Other online sites that sent players to the WSOP includes ParadisePoker.com, PartyPoker.com, and UltimateBet.com.

Online casinos start offering satellites for the WSOP months before it begins. Winning a seat early takes quite a bit of pressure off your shoulders. You can then compete for additional seats, and if you win another satellite, you can use your satellite chips to play more events at the World Series.

3. Win a One-Table Satellite for a $1,000-$5,000 WSOP Seat

In addition to satellites for the championship event, the Horseshoe spreads one-table satellites for all of the other WSOP tournaments. Every day of the week during the Series, you can play limit hold'em and no-limit hold'em satellites. The Shoe usually starts spreading satellites for its non-hold'em events the day before the tournament, and runs them around the clock until just before the tournament begins.

4. Win a Two-Tier Double Shootout Satellite at the Horseshoe

Early in January the Horseshoe begins offering its two-tier satellites. After the Series begins, the Shoe increases the number of two-tier satellites from one or two a day to ten or more a day.

5. Win a Super Satellite at the Horseshoe

When the World Series begins, the Shoe starts its super satellite program. The super satellites that are run just prior to the start of the championship event usually are so big that they award as many as fifteen seats each.

6. Win a Seat in a Super Satellite via a One-Table Satellite

The Horseshoe starts running its $50 one-table satellites for a seat in a super satellite when it begins its super satellite program. In this program, the top two finalists in the one-table satellite are awarded a $225 seat in a super satellite.

7. Win a One-Table Satellite for a $10,000 Seat

Usually during the second week of the Series, the Horseshoe starts running its one-table satellites for a $10,000 seat into the championship event. These one-tables cost $1,030 to enter and award a seat plus some cash to the winner. The rounds last twenty minutes each and you begin with $4,000 in satellite chips, so these one-tables have a lot of play to them.

About midway through the Series, demand for these one-table satellites increases, and they are held several times a day.

"The last three or four days before the championship event begins," Tom adds, "people seem to go into a feeding frenzy. Players who haven't won a seat start scrambling to get into these one-table satellites for the Big One. Even players who already have won a seat like to play these satellites. Considering the low vig and the amount of play, we consider them a good value for the money."

When it gets to crunch time, a day or two before the main event begins, the Horseshoe runs a lot more $1,030 buy-in one-table satellites. The day before the Big One starts, these one-tables run around the clock through the night.

The morning of the main event, you'll hear the satellite coordinator continually announce, "One more satellite!" Then a very interesting thing happens in the last hour before the Big One starts. Twenty-minute rounds are reduced to seven- or even five-minute rounds. Naturally the play goes much faster because the satellite has to end by the time the championship event starts.

"I've even played crunch-time satellites where the blinds increased on every single hand!" Tom says.

In a deal like this, the big blind is the optimal seat you could draw, because after taking the small blind, you'll have the button and will be able to see as many hands as possible. The satellite probably will be over before you have to take the blinds again. Of course you'll probably have to move in with a hand before that. You'll have to play very aggressively in a satellite like this.

8. Win a "Last Chance" Satellite the Morning of the Big One

Now let's talk about "last-chance" time. Just when you think there's no chance whatsoever that another satellite will be held, the satellite director at the Horseshoe will announce, "We have time for one more satellite! If we can get ten players down here right now, you can play one hand for a satellite seat, winner take all."

Tom adds: "I've even seen some world champions flip out $1,000 each to win a $10,000 toss of the coin."

In this one-hand showdown, the dealer high-cards for the button, deals the cards to all players, and then deals all the community cards. Whoever shows down the best hand wins the seat.

"Actually, this is the most exciting satellite played at the World Series," Brad observes. "People will be standing five deep to try to see who wins it. Everybody loves it. And then, guess what? They'll run another one!"

Even if you haven't learned your satellite lessons from this book, here's a satellite you can win. And you don't care how tough the lineup is!

9. Win a Seat in an On-Land Tournament That Awards a WSOP Seat to the Winner

Several on-land casinos run major tournaments that award cash plus a seat in a WSOP tournament to the winner. These tournaments may award a $1,500 seat, $2,500 seat, or even an entry into the Big One. The cost of the seat is subtracted from the total prize pool.

Probably the most prestigious event at which you can win a WSOP seat is the Shooting Stars tournament sponsored by Bay 101 in San Jose, California. It is a one-of-a-kind super satellite with a lot of money and prestige at stake. The casino rolls out the red carpet for everyone, even providing limousine service from the nearby airport. Limited to 150 players, the tournament costs $1,500 to enter and usually pays nine spots.

The tournament begins with fifteen tables of ten players, each with one "shooting star" assigned to each table. The casino selects the shooting stars, which are world-class players and usually former world poker champions or renowned cash players. The house awards a $1,500 bounty to any player who shoots down a star.

"Brad and I have been selected as shooting stars several times," Tom notes. "If a star knocks out another star, he gets the $1,500 bounty. And if a star wins the tournament, he also wins his own bounty money."

The top three finishers win WSOP seats plus a cash award. The tournament lasts for two days, with the final table being played on the second day. Carlos Mortensen, the 2001 World Champion of Poker, won his seat in the WSOP championship event at the Shooting Stars.

10. Run Satellites in Your Home Game

You can run your own satellites in home games. Eighteen firefighters from the East held a series of satellites in 2003, and then put one man into the championship event. The other seventeen firefighters each had a piece of the action and attended the Series to root for their representative.

"I talked with a few of these men," Brad notes, "and they said they were having the time of their lives."

Home-game satellites also could be held for WSOP tournaments that cost less than the main event.

What If You Don't Win a Seat?

Another way to get into a WSOP tournament is by selling pieces of your action. In 2000 when Cowboy Wolford came in third in the $2,000 pot-limit hold'em event, he sold 50 percent of his action to twenty backers for $100 each. Each shareholder received 2.5 percent of his net win. Wolford won over $60,000, so each of his shareholders made a $1,500 return on a $100 investment.

Or you can follow the example of world-class players such as T.J. Cloutier who have a single backer for all or some of the events in the World Series. Of course you have to first establish a track record as a winning tournament player. And you don't get to take home your total win. Usually, you only receive 50 percent of your net win.

Your Last Resort

Your last resort for getting into the World Series of Poker is brutal: you can plunk down $10,000 out of your pocket and buy your way in.

"I had to resort to that method in 1991," Brad

admits, "but only because I didn't win either of the one-table satellites I played the morning of the championship event."

To save you from this ugly alternative, we are giving you the winning advice you need to win your way into the World Series of Poker via a satellite. Of course you can also use these strategies to win your way into almost any major tournament. Almost every casino that holds a big tournament also offers satellites for each event in its series of tournaments.

How Satellites Work

2

Many players start their tournament day at the satellite table.

"Rather than this being a $1,000 buy-in tournament today," Brad says, "I think of it as a $115 buy-in tournament that starts right here at the satellite. If I win here, I'll be playing a $115 buy-in tournament, not a $1,000 buy-in tournament."

If it's a $2,000 tournament you're hoping to win a seat for, the satellite will cost you around $225. If you win it, you will have changed the actual buy-in for the tournament from $2,000 to $225. Then you will have the chance to parlay your $225 investment into $100,000 or more.

Usually, however, you should plan to play satellites a day or two prior to the tournament. Although some people do play a one-table satellite the morning of the tournament, you're usually better off playing them a day or so in advance since they require so much energy. If you win it, then have to turn around and play the event that same day, you'll lose a little something in the process. Today's satellite scene includes one-table satellites, satellites for bigger satellites, two-tier or double-shootouts, super satellites, and online satellites.

In this section we describe the setup, structure, and cost of satellites, and give you other information on each type of satellite. We also answer many questions that newcomers ask about satellites.

One-Table Satellites at the Horseshoe and Other Casinos

Suppose you want to play a $2,000 limit hold'em tournament at the World Series of Poker. You don't have $2,000 in your jeans, so you're considering ponying up the $225 satellite entry fee for a $2,000 limit hold'em satellite at Binion's Horseshoe. But before you sit down, there are still a lot of questions you need to answer.

How Do You Buy into a Satellite?

You find the satellite director, and tell him you want to play a satellite. He will tell you the table to go to. When you get there, you'll draw for a seat, sit down in your seat number, and after all the players are there and the table is full, the director will collect the money for the satellite. Unlike buying into a tournament, they usually wait until the satellite fills before they take your money.

Can You Change Your Mind if You Find Yourself at a Table with Intimidating Players?

Yes. If you change your mind before the table fills up, you can withdraw and wait for another satellite that you like. In fact, until the first hand is dealt, you can give up your seat.

"I have even sat down at a table where I didn't like the lineup," Brad reports, "and when somebody came looking for a seat, I told him he could have my seat."

You can even give up your seat after the satellite has started if no one at the table objects.

Being able to choose your table in a one-table satellite is an advantage. You can determine whether the lineup at that table is a good one or a bad one for you to play, and then either go ahead and play it or wait for the next one. However, keep in mind that you can't choose your table in a super satellite, where tables are assigned randomly.

How Many Chips Do You Get at the Start?

For a $2,000 tournament satellite, you're going to get between $600 and $800 in chips, usually $800.

What Limits Do You Start at and How Fast Do They Go Up?

The limits usually begin at $15/$30. The blinds usually are $10/$15 and go up every fifteen minutes.

Do the Limits Double Every Round?

No. In the second level, the limits go up to $30/$60, and after this level, the clock stops, and the dealer buys each player's $5 chips. For every five $5 chip a player has, he receives a $25 chip. Some players will be left with one, two, three, or four $5 chips, and these are raced off. Here's how it works: The dealer shuffles the cards and gives all the players with odd chips one card per chip. The player with the highest card receives a $25 chip from the odd chip pile. The player with the next highest card receives a $25 chip as well, and so forth until the odd chips are gone. No player can win more than one $25 chip, and if there are still a couple of odd $5 chips left at the end of the race, they are removed from play.

In the third level, the limits rise to $50/$100 with $25/$50 blinds. The limits usually double in the next round, going up from $50/$100 to $100/$200, and sometimes the limits jump to $200/$400 in the fourth round. Other times they rise more slowly with a $150/$300 round. From there the limits rise to $300/$600 and $400/$800. There may be a bigger jump occasionally, but the first four levels usually are the same from year to year.

How Soon Does a Player Usually Get Knocked Out? At Which Level?

Someone usually gets knocked out in no-limit satellites during the first level. In a limit hold'em satellite with $15-$30 limits, it's very hard to lose $800 in chips in fifteen minutes. It isn't impossible, but it is difficult. In limit satellites, you might lose one player, or two at the most, in the second level. In the third level, players start dropping quicker.

How Long Does a One-Table Limit Satellite Last?

Limit satellites usually are over in an hour to an hour and a half. In general, they end some time around the fourth, fifth, or sixth level.

How About a No-Limit Hold'em Satellite?

No-limit hold'em satellites are designed to last about the same length of time—60 to 90 minutes. Of course, more players can be knocked out earlier because you can bet all your chips, whereas in limit hold'em satellites, your chips are more protected.

How Are Seven-Card Stud Satellites Structured?

Seven-card stud satellites play similar to limit hold'em satellites, except that there are eight players instead of ten. Seven-card stud, razz, and stud eight-or-better are all eight-player satellites. It costs a little bit more to enter them, because there are fewer players. Very few people go out in the first level of a stud satellite; usually you don't lose one until the second level. In the third level the players start dropping, and by the fourth level you're usually down to three or four players. By the fifth level, the play is normally three-handed or heads-up.

When Should You Start Playing Satellites for the World Series?

"I like to start playing the double-shootouts the first of January at the Horseshoe," says McEvoy.

But what if you don't live in Las Vegas? Many casinos around the world, including Internet casinos, offer a lot of satellites. Some online cardrooms start them as early as January. You could even get a casino near you to run a World Series satellite. Although not every casino runs satellites for the championship event, they often will run smaller buy-in satellites for events such as the $2,000 limit hold'em event at the WSOP.

Casinos also run satellites for seats in the World Poker Open and other major tournaments.

Bellagio even runs a satellite for the $25,000 buy-in championship event at the WPO. No matter where you are, and no matter what the stakes are, you can always find a satellite online.

One-Table Satellites to Win an Entry into a Super Satellite

During the 2003 World Series of Poker, the Horseshoe introduced a new type of satellite: one-table satellites that awarded seats for a super satellite. The buy-in was $50 and the satellite advanced two players to the $225 super satellite. Players started with $300 in chips and rounds lasted ten minutes each, so the house cranked them out pretty fast. The Shoe kept $50 and awarded the $225 entry fee into a super satellite to each of the two finalists. Designed for quicker play, these satellites usually lasted for only forty minutes.

Since the Horseshoe ran two super satellites a day, some people played two of these $50 satellites a day in an effort to win two super-satellite seats for a total investment of $100. Many players played a super satellite the same day that they won one of these one-table events. Several players went on to win a super satellite and advanced to the $10,000 championship event for an investment of only $50.

Two-Tier Double-Shootout Satellites at the World Series of Poker

During the World Series of Poker, Binion's Horseshoe offers two-tier satellites that award a $10,000 entry into the championship event. In these double shootouts, ten players pay $125 ($100 entry fee plus $25 vig) each to play the first tier, a ten-handed no-limit hold'em one-table satellite. Each player receives $4,000 in chips. The twenty-minute rounds begin with blinds of $25/$25 and progress to $25/$50, $50/$200, $100/$200, $150/$300, $200/$400, $300/$600 and $500/$1,000, if it lasts that long. The satellite usually ends during the $300-$600 level.

The ten winners of the first-tier satellites then assemble to play the second tier. Each finalist receives $4,000 in chips. The rounds last thirty minutes each, with one extra round added, which gives players plenty of time of play. The casino awards the winner a $10,000 seat for the championship event, and also gives $300 to the second-place finisher and $200 to third place. We consider these satellites to be a good investment, despite the $25 juice.

"The second leg of the double shootouts are about the longest one-table satellites I've ever played," Tom observes, "because they give you plenty of chips and lots of time to play."

The Horseshoe begins offering these two-tier satellites in early January and usually runs them through the middle of the Series. The satellites generally begin at 2:00 p.m. and end around 6:00 p.m. You receive a receipt for your win and then put your name on the schedule for the second tier of the satellite, which usually is held on a Saturday afternoon. As it gets closer to the WSOP, the Horseshoe starts spreading two or three two-tier events daily.

Because you get a lot more play in these events than you do in many other one-table satellites, you can almost skip playing the first round without hurting your chances of winning it. With the blinds at only $25/$25, $4,000 in chips to play, longer rounds, and no significant money in the pot, you have no reason to even play a hand during the first round unless you're dealt something very strong. You usually do not lose a single player in the first two rounds, but after the blinds rise to $50-$100, the satellite starts going strong.

Many players have won seats into the $10,000 event through these double-shootout satellites. Tomer Benvenisti parlayed his double-shootout satellite win into $320,000 when he placed fifth in the Big One in 2003. Both Daugherty and McEvoy won their entries into the Big One in 2002 through a two-tier double-shootout satellite.

"If you're lucky, you can become a multiple

winner before the Series begins," Daugherty notes. "When you win your seat in advance, it takes a lot of pressure off your shoulders."

Super Satellites at On-Land Casinos

Unlike one-table satellites for which you post a single buy-in, super satellites usually are rebuy tournaments. The structure of super satellites is unique in that you receive the same amount of chips as the cost of your buy-in. For example, a super satellite at the WSOP costs $225 to enter. You start out with $200 in chips and the rounds last for twenty minutes. You may rebuy for the first three levels of play and add on at the end of the rebuy period. The blinds start at $5/$10, then progress to $10/$20 and $15/$30. After three levels of play, the nickel chips ($5) are raced off.

At the end of the rebuy period, you are allowed to add on if you have $200 or less in chips. You can also take two add-ons, no matter what your chip count is. After all the rebuys and add-ons have been completed, there is a short break, after which the blinds rise to $25/$50 at the fourth level. Some people don't even enter the super satellite until the break—they then buy in for $800 and start playing at the $25/$50 level.

After the $100/$200 level, the blinds start

doubling, going up to $200/$400, then usually $300/$600 (but sometimes $400/$800), and then $500/$1000. In other words, the structure is faster in the later stages than it is in the earlier stages. (A better structure for the players would be something like $200/$400, $300/$600, $400/$800, and $600/$1200.)

The number of tournament seats that are awarded through a super satellite depends entirely on the number of buy-ins, rebuys and add-ons in the satellite. For example if the super satellite fund is $37,000, three seats for the $10,000 WSOP championship event are awarded. In this scenario, the winners also would win some cash, ensuring that their entire expenses have been paid and providing them with some toke money, in case they wish to tip the dealers. The three winners in this example would probably get $10,300, with fourth place and maybe fifth place also receiving some cash. Usually, they'll pay anywhere from seven to nine spots, although they normally don't go to nine spots unless the field is huge. Sometimes there is barely enough extra cash for the top three spots.

The super satellite ends when the number of players left at the table equals the number of seats available in the prize pool. Regardless of your chip count—whether you have two chips or $20,000 in chips—if you are one of the three or four (or whatever the number of tournament seats being awarded) finalists, you will win a seat in the main tournament. Sadly, bad things sometimes happen when you get very close to the end.

"One time at the Four Queens Classic," Brad says, "I was playing a super satellite in which they were giving five seats for the $5,000 championship event. With six of us left, I was second in chips and looked down at pocket aces. The big stack called my raise and busted me! Naturally, I didn't win a seat."

Satellites at Online Casinos

For the first time in history, a large number of people won seats in the championship event at the 2003 WSOP on the Internet via online casinos such as PokerStars.com, PartyPoker.com, and ParadisePoker.com. Players had the advantage of playing satellites in their comfort zone at home, insulated from the sometimes intimidating atmosphere of live play.

"I saw more people that I didn't recognize at the WSOP in 2003 than all of the twenty other World Series that I have played combined," McEvoy observes. "In one of the $500 satellites that I played, I didn't recognize a single face!"

One of the most important upsides of playing online satellites is that you get to see a lot more hands than you see in on-land satellites in the same time period. A fifteen-minute round online is roughly equivalent to playing a thirty-minute round on-land. One reason for this is because you don't have to wait for the dealer to manually shuffle the deck. A cyber dealer automatically deals the cards at the start of each new hand. Also, players can't delay the game as much because the cyber clock automatically gives them sixty seconds to act; after that, their hands are folded. The cyber dealer never misdeals and always cuts the pots correctly and instantly.

The typical online limit hold'em satellite gives you $1,500 in chips with fifteen-minute rounds. The blinds start at $10/$20 and progress to $15/$30, $20/$40, $30/$60, and so on. When tables break up, a cyber floorperson physically moves players and their chips to a new table instantly. In online satellites and tournaments where there is more than one table, you play hand-for-hand to eliminate one more player and start the final table, but it doesn't take as long as it does in on-land casinos.

If you need to leave the game for a few minutes, you click the "sit out" button and the program automatically folds your hand so that the game doesn't slow down. If you stay out for too long, you will hear a nasty little beep and after a countdown of sixty seconds, the cyber dealer will fold your hand. But it only does that once—you have to click "I'm back" or it will continue folding your hands, noting that you are "sitting out." In tournaments, you are automatically dealt in, but your hand is folded when it's your turn to act.

Although you have about the same time to play in online satellites as you do in on-land satellites, you actually receive more hands. The advantage of receiving more hands is that the cards have more time to even out, thus reducing the luck factor. In other words, every player usually gets a chance to catch his fair share of good cards. Getting more hands to look at is beneficial to the better players because they have more opportunities to practice their advanced skills.

"If you're not touching a lot of cards," Daugherty notes, "you'll have to flip a coin for all your chips with a marginal hand, maybe a small pair against two overcards, to determine your fate. When you get to look at thirty hands versus twenty hands, it makes a big difference in how many hands you can play."

Internet poker may be superior to live poker in some ways, but it also has its downside. For one thing, you can't look at the players.

"It's kind of nice to be able to look a player in the eyeballs and get a feel for where he's at," Daugherty says. "A lot of times in live games, your opponents give you free information that they can't give you online. For example, in an on-land satellite, a player might turn up his cards for you to see. 'Look what I folded,' he might say trying to impress you with his good play."

Or he might flash his cards. Online players cannot accidentally expose their cards. Nor can they act out of turn. Sometimes a player will prematurely fold his hand when he's in the big blind, but the program won't let him fold. "Are you sure you want to fold?" the cyber dealer asks. In essence, the program protects you and your opponents from your own mistakes.

Some people have voiced their concern about the possibility of collusion in online poker games. The collusion issue is greatly diminished in tournament play because the lineup at tournament tables is determined randomly, which makes it almost impossible for "friends" to be seated at the same table.

Online Satellites to Win a Seat in a Bigger Satellite

In recent years, several online casinos have begun offering small buy-in no-limit hold'em satellites from which the winners advance to a much larger satellite that awards $10,000 seats for the championship event at the WSOP. At Pokerstars.com, the entry fee for the first tier was $39 and awarded $615 seats into the second tier. In 2003 the $39 satellites were multi-table events rather than one-table events, as they are in the Horseshoe's two-tier events. Further, players did not have to win a seat in the first tier in order to play in the second tier—you could skip playing the $39 preliminary satellites and pay your way into the $615 second tier if you wanted to.

The online sites accepted as many players as possible for the preliminary events and offered as many $615 seats as the prize pool allowed. They used the same procedure for the second tier and awarded as many $10,000 seats as the prize pool allowed. At both levels, then, the number of entries determined the number of seats awarded. For example, if there were $6,150 in the prize pool of the first tier, ten people would win seats into the second tier.

In the two-tier online satellites at PokerStars.com, players began with $1,500 in satellite chips and played fifteen-minute rounds. In on-land casinos, play stops as soon as the number of players left in action is the same as the number of seats being awarded. In online casinos, the satellite is played to its conclusion, primarily because that is the way their software is designed.

"When I know that I've won a seat," Brad notes, "I have a unique play—I move in on every hand. I know that I can't win any additional money, so I want to get it over with quickly. Several other players do the same thing."

Because both the preliminary $39 satellite and the $615 satellite are multi-table events, they are similar to on-land super satellites except that no rebuys are allowed. In essence if you win both tiers of these online super satellites, you win a $10,000 seat into the Big One. Chris Moneymaker parlayed $39 into $2.5 million when he won the championship event at the 2003 World Series of Poker after winning the first and second legs of an online two-tier satellite at Pokerstars.com — probably the biggest parlay in WSOP history.

"In my opinion," McEvoy says, "it's the wave of the future. Internet sites will be sending more and more players to the World Series through multi-table satellite programs."

"I played several online satellites in 2003," Daugherty adds, "especially on PokerStars, where they gave away frequent player points. I played one freeroll satellite that had 348 players, giving away three seats in the championship event at the World Series. Unfortunately I came seventh and got back $500 rather than a $10,000 seat. But at least I won something for my efforts."

Other Aspects of Online Poker

With the Absence of Body Language in Online Poker, What Other Types of Tells Can You Rely On?

For one thing, you can observe the quickness of your opponents' check responses. Suppose you pause for a second when you check, and the action automatically goes past the opponent to your left very quickly. You know that he clicked his check button before you acted. Therefore you know there's a good chance that he doesn't have anything. Knowing this, if you bet on the next flop card, there's a good chance that you'll win the pot.

Or let's say that you want a free card. You can just let the screen blink and blink and blink, as though you're thinking about what to do. Then you check. In that case it often is likely that your opponents will also check.

"Yes, but when I make a bet on PokerStars.com and there's a pause, I'm usually getting raised!" Brad observes.

How About Keeping a "Book" on Your Opponents?

"I take notes all the time online so that I can keep track of whether 'Jane Plain' is a good or bad player and so on," Brad notes. "I'm always updating a log of information on all of my opponents."

Can You Play Anonymously by Using an Alias?

Of course, and many players use colorful playing names.

"It is fun to play under a pseudonym," Tom

remarks. "But I never use one on PokerStars.com because I am a spokesman for that site."

If you are a well-known player, it can be to your disadvantage to use your real name. You also can disguise your gender with your playing name. Women who believe they have been the victims of gender bias in live poker games can assume a name such as Gorilla Gus, for example.

"On the other hand," Brad observes, "I know that two of my online opponents with female names—'I Am a Stripper' and 'Brenda B'—are men."

How Do You Buy Into an Online Satellite?

You can buy in with either cash or frequent player points. To set up an account with UltimateBet, for example, go to www.UltimateBet.com, download the software, and install it on your computer. You can have an alias with a unique password. Then you will have to show your email address so that you can buy chips. In order to buy chips, you will need to set up an account with an online vendor that can convert funds into online cash.

"I use neteller.com," Tom notes. "All online poker sites use NETELLER, which enables direct deposits to and withdrawals from your bank. It takes about four business days."

Sites used to take credit cards, but they got a lot of heat from the government. In addition, gambling sites will no longer accept payment through PayPal.com. At this time, NETELLER.com is the main way to deposit money.

When Can You Sign Up for an Online Satellite?

You usually can sign up for a satellite up to an hour before it starts. Games normally are posted a week or so in advance. When you play cash games online, you earn bonus points that you can use to play freeroll tournaments.

Is the Vigorish the Same in Online and On-Land Casinos?

No. It is less at online casinos. For example, $100 online satellites usually have a $9 vig for a total cost of $109. At on-land casinos the vig for a $100 satellite is $15 to $25 for a total cost of between $115-$125. The vig for a $50 online satellite is usually $5, whereas it's usually $10 on-land.

One-Table Satellites: Important Factors to Consider

by Brad Daugherty

3

Before you begin playing one-table satellites, you should design a game plan that includes how many one-tables you intend to play, when you will play them, how much money you will need to budget for your satellite play, and other factors. Included in this section are our opinions on these important aspects of playing one-table satellites.

When Should You Play One-Table Satellites?

Let us ask you this question: How does it affect your emotional state when you start your tournament day by playing a satellite or two and you lose?

Tom responds this way: "When I know for sure that I'm going to play the tournament whether or not I win a seat for it, I don't want to play more than one satellite, two at the most. Losing a satellite just before I start playing a tournament puts me in a bad frame of mind. Of course if I'm fortunate enough to win, then it's the other way around. Now I'm elated, my confidence is high, my morale is boosted. However if I'm not planning to play the tournament if I don't win a seat, it doesn't affect me one way or the other except that I'm disappointed."

Tom and I both prefer playing a satellite or two the day before a tournament that we know we're going to play anyway. That way you can come in fresh the next day with a new frame of mind, after a good night's sleep and some time to shrug off a satellite loss.

In 1991 I played two one-table satellites the morning of the $10,000 World Series of Poker championship tournament. I got heads-up in both of them and got drawn out both times. I tried to make a deal with one of my heads-up opponents, an Australian who had to pay United States tax on his tournament wins. He had more chips that I did, so I offered him a really good deal, forty percent of me in the Big One.

He could've done extremely well if he'd taken my deal, but instead he won the seat, which ended up netting him about $7,000 after taxes. Since I was the first $1 million-dollar winner at the WSOP, he would have won around $400,000 from me if he had taken the deal.

But here's my main point: After two satellite defeats, I was so deflated that I almost decided not to play. Luckily, at the last moment I went ahead and bought into the tournament. In fact I was the last player to buy into the 1991 World Series of Poker championship event. Fortunately I was also the last player with chips at the championship table.

Suppose you're planning to play a tournament on Tuesday and you decide to play a satellite for it that morning. You probably should play only one satellite the morning of a tournament you're planning to enter, or two at the most. Playing a satellite just before the tournament lengthens your tournament day considerably. If you're planning to play two satellites the morning of a noon event, you should plan to arrive at the casino at nine o'clock to give yourself enough time.

We believe that it is better to play a satellite or two the day before the tournament. Some one-table satellites have super-fast structures immediately prior to the tournament. The closer it is to the hour the tournament begins, the less time there is to complete satellites for it. Therefore the satellite director sometimes will change the rounds from fifteen minutes to five minutes, for example.

Now you're in a real shoot-out for a satellite seat. We recommend that you always ask the floor person how long the rounds will be before you enter a satellite.

How Many One-Table Satellites Should You Play?

The overall number of one-table satellites you play is directly related to your satellite bankroll. Usually, I will allot a certain amount of money to play satellites. Suppose I budget enough to play ten satellites during the entire tournament. I can either play all ten satellites in one day, or I might decide that as soon as I win one I'll quit for that day, buy into the tournament I want to play, and go home.

You don't want to play too many one-table satellites in the same day because you risk burning yourself out. We suggest no more than two or three. If you play more than that, instead of a $1,000 buy-in tournament costing you $1,060, it's going to cost you about 1 1/3 times that amount if you don't win a seat. In other words, you want to avoid over investing in satellite play for one particular tournament.

Tom believes that if you're going to play the tournament regardless of whether you win a satellite for it, you should play only two satellites. However, when you win a satellite, the satellite chips that you earn can usually be used for any tournament that you want to enter. Therefore, if there are other tournaments that you're also planning to play, it doesn't matter quite as much how many satellites you play because you're playing for seats in multiple events. If you are not going to play the tournament unless you win a satellite seat, we recommend that you play no more than three satellites maximum for it.

How Much Money Should You Budget to Play Satellites?

One factor that affects your satellite budget is whether you're planning to buy in to the tournament regardless of whether you win a satellite seat. A lot of players come to the WSOP with a fixed amount of money they're willing to invest in satellites. If they're disciplined enough, they do not exceed their predetermined budget. If they aren't, they're liable to catch "WSOP fever," in which some of them go through their entire budgets and then borrow as much money as they can to try to win a seat in the Big One.

If you're going to buy into the tournament anyhow, the purpose of your satellite play is simply to try to get in it cheaply. Suppose you're planning to play ten tournaments during the Series. If you're playing good satellite strategy, over a period of time you should come out on the top side of your satellite budget. If you're running good, you might even win seats for a bunch of them. If you know that you're going to enter ten events, you might want to budget yourself for twenty satellites, two per event. As we said earlier, if you're not going to play an event unless you win a seat for it, you should play no more than three satellites for it. That way, you won't get too buried. If you're going to play the event anyway, you don't want to have more invested in it and your satellite play than you can hope to get out of the tournament if you at least come into the money.

If you have budgeted for twenty satellites, it doesn't matter whether you play three satellites for the same event—it's just a part of your overall satellite play. You might arrive in Vegas four days before the first tournament that you want to play in the WSOP, for example, and play nothing but satellites. A lot of serious tournament players do this. Some players come to the WSOP every year just to play satellites. These satellite specialists then play only one or two tournaments at the most, and sell the greater share of their satellite chips.

Note that if you decide to play ten satellites total in an on-land casino, you probably will need to budget about 10 to 15 percent more money in today's economic conditions than you would have a decade ago. Of course, you hope that the tournament you're going to enter when you win your satellite seat will have 10 to 15 percent more entries than it had ten years ago. In fact many of today's bigger buy-in tournaments have doubled and even tripled in size, especially no-limit hold'em events.

One reason for this growth is that the online satellite system has given players many more opportunities to practice their no-limit hold'em game. We also believe that *Championship No-Limit & Pot-Limit Hold'em* has played a major part in the expansion of no-limit tournaments by helping its readers to overcome the fear of playing no-limit poker. I've noticed that whereas players used to be more timid in their play, these days they're not afraid to put their money in and mix it up. The irony is that limit hold'em used to be the most popular satellite and tournament game. That has changed: Today everybody seems to want to play no-limit hold'em. As a consequence, no-limit hold'em tournaments often have larger fields than limit hold'em events.

How Do You Get Paid When You Win a Satellite?

Some casinos will give you a voucher that you use to enter the tournament. Other times you will be paid in tournament chips, and sometimes, you receive a small amount of cash in addition to the tournament chips. When you play a satellite for a $5,000 or $10,000 tournament (usually the championship event in the tournament), it is generally understood that you must play the event for which you have won a satellite seat. However if you already have won a seat for that event, you can take chips instead of the voucher. After winning their first seat in a super satellite, some players—usually satellite specialists—enter additional super satellites and sell the tournament chips they win for cash. Note that you cannot buy into any of the World Series tournaments with cash—you must buy in with tournament chips. You can purchase these chips from the cage or buy them from another player. Immediately after the championship event begins at the WSOP, tournament chips are devalued. Imagine how you might feel if you had forgotten to sell an extra $500 chip! Of course you will have a nice souvenir.

The vouchers that you receive for events other than the championship tournament usually are generic, and you can use them for any event with a buy-in that is the same as the voucher. Except for the championship event, vouchers usually are negotiable and sometimes are sold at a slight discount, usually by satellite specialists.

Should You Tip Satellite Dealers?

Yes, unless the tip is built into the vig. Normally the tip is $20. If two people split the satellite, they'll usually leave $10 each—unless a certain percentage of the vig is reserved by the casino for dealer gratuities. Always ask.

If nothing is withheld for the dealers, I usually tip a quarter ($25). I look at how long the dealer has been in the box. If a dealer has had to deal longer than usual, he's entitled to a little more. If the satellite is over early, I don't leave as much.

As in all of poker, the dealer's prowess usually affects the amount that players tip. If a dealer has dealt the hands quickly and efficiently, most players are prone to tip more. One percent of the buy-in would be considered a small tip; three percent would be a big tip. Another thing I've done, is to offer the dealer a small percentage of my action in the main tournament if I win my way into it through the satellite. This is in lieu of a toke. That way they get to gamble along with me. A lot of them seem to like this idea because, instead of a small tip, they have a chance at winning a lot more money.

One-Table Satellites at On-Land Casinos

Tom McEvoy and I believe that a satellite should cost the lowest price possible in order to ensure a good deal for players and a reasonable profit for the house. For this reason, we favor barebones satellites that players can enter for a minimum cash outlay with no extra cash being awarded for first place. In an ideal scenario, a $1,000 satellite would cost each player $115. The house would hold $90 juice and award $1,060 to the winner, just enough to cover the cost of the tournament and the entry fee.

The vig the house is taking today is more than it was when I started playing poker full-time in 1987. Unfortunately it has continued to increase over the years. It seems to me that some of the Las Vegas casinos set a precedent for the amount of the vig and as a consequence, it has continually risen. Hopefully it will cap soon.

Nowadays, with the increased vig, you need to win one out of eight satellites you enter to break about even. In a sense, you got one extra satellite buy-in when the vig was lower. In the houses' defense, running satellites is labor intensive and expenses have risen. Wages are somewhat higher, although dealers still heavily depend on tokes from players. And of course, not all casinos charge the same vigorish for satellites. Some charge less and some charge more. It doesn't cost the casino a whole lot more to run a one-table satellite for a higher buy-in event than for a lower buy-in event, but they usually take a higher vigorish from the $1,000 satellites than they do from the $300 satellites, for example. The $1,000 satellites usually take about fifteen minutes longer to play, and the casino is certainly entitled to cover its extra labor costs. By comparison, if the house holds $160 on a $1,000 satellite, how much would we be paying if the house held the same percentage on a $10,000 satellite? The answer is $1,600. And if the house held the same proportion that it does for a $1,000 satellite, the casino would hold $16,000 if it ran a $100,000 satellite.

Actually, the buy-in for a $10,000 satellite usually is $1,030 and the house holds $150 to $200. The irony is that, percentage-wise, the vig is still quite reasonable for the $10,000 satellites.

Satellites for Small Buy-In Tournaments

The vig for smaller buy-in satellites is much higher in relation to the vig for bigger buy-in tournaments. At this point in my tournament career, I can afford to simply buy in to them. But if you're just starting to play tournament poker and you're on a limited bankroll, the smaller buy-in satellites are a good place to start. One-table satellites offer you great opportunities to practice your tournament skills and playing them can put you in the right frame of mind for playing the particular tournament you're planning to enter. Playing one-table satellites is similar to playing at the final table of the tournament (except that each player begins with an equal amount of chips), so it's a good place to practice your final-table play, including shorthanded play because if you win or place high in the satellite, you eventually will be playing three-handed and heads-up. One-table satellites are still the way to go for the majority of low-limit tournament players.

Other Considerations

In our opinion, however, we're close to the breaking point as far as how much more juice players can be charged and still make one-table satellites worthwhile to play. Better players need to have a positive profit expectation in their one-table satellite play, but things are getting to the point these days where satellites for the lower buy-in tournaments are not a viable option.

A very good one-table satellite player hopes to win one out of four or five satellites he enters. Even winning one out of six is above average for an excellent satellite player. If a good player wins one out of five, he is still making a profit, but certainly not as much as he used to be able to make. Don't get us wrong, however, because a good player still can make a profit at one-table satellites. It's simply more difficult to do these days because of the increased juice.

There are players that we call "professional satellite players" or "satellite specialists" who play satellite after satellite and play hardly any tournaments because they are making a nice profit at their satellite play. But some casinos now are locking you in on one-table satellites—that is, you are required to play the tournament for the first satellite that you enter, particularly for $5,000 and higher tournaments. After your first win, you can sell your satellite chips.

Another factor that professional satellite players must consider is the new model of "winning a satellite to enter a satellite." In this case, when you win the preliminary satellite you are automatically entered into the main satellite. If you win that satellite, you are rewarded with a seat in the big tournament. This is exactly what 2003 World Champion Chris Moneymaker did to enter and then win the championship event at the World Series of Poker.

The Upside

These figures might lead some players to believe that they would be better off playing in a live game to earn their tournament entry than they would be playing in a satellite. However, unless you're extremely lucky, you can't earn enough in a $10/$20 game in one hour to pay for a $1,000 tournament entry, whereas you can do it in the hour or so that it takes to play a satellite. Again, the advantage of playing a satellite is that you only have to risk $115 to $125 and play for sixty to ninety minutes to win a seat in a $1,000 tournament. Although on-land casinos have increased the juice on satellites, playing satellites is still the way to go if you don't have enough money for a tournament buy-in.

One-Table Satellites at Online Casinos

A satellite for a $1,000 online tournament costs about $109 at most Internet casino sites, which is less juice that most on-land casinos charge. Of course online casinos have no dealer payroll expenses, so they don't have the overhead that brick-and-mortar on-land casinos have. If I win one out of nine online satellites, I will break about even. If I win one out of eight on-land satellites, I will break about even. In other words, I'm getting one more satellite for my money online.

You also get a lot more hands to play per level because the cards are dealt so quickly. Naturally I like paying less vig and having more hands to play in the same time frame that it would take me to play in a live casino satellite. But the biggest perk is that I get to look at fifteen to twenty more hands in an online satellite. The advantage to being dealt more hands is that it increases the skill factor and decreases the luck factor, thus giving you more chance for the cards to even out. And that is why I tend to play lots of satellites online these days.

Satellite Bargains

The biggest bargains in one-table on-land satellites are satellites for the $1,500 buy-in and higher tournaments. A very playable one-table satellite for a $1,570 tournament is one that costs $170 to enter. The house keeps $100 and gives the winner a $1,570 seat plus $30 in cash. In typical major tournaments, the casino awards satellite chips to the winner. Each chip is worth $500, and they are negotiable. If you're playing for a $1,570 seat, the casino usually gives you three satellite chips and $100 cash, which can be used to cover the vigorish as well as tip money. You normally start with $600 in chips for a total of $6,000 chips in play.

Bellagio offered a bargain at its Festa al Lago tournament in 2003. The casino held a super satellite for its $5,000 no-limit hold'em main event that cost $540 with no rebuys. Players began with $1,000 in chips. This set a new precedent: A big buy-in, freezeout satellite for a major tournament the day before the championship event was played. In our opinion, this super satellite was a reasonable deal for the players in that they had a shot to win a $5,000 seat, received a lot of play, and only had to pay $40 vig for the satellite. Whereas I passed on playing Bellagio's one-table satellites because of the vig, this super satellite was a bargain. With so much play, better satellite players had a chance to use their skills, knowing that if the cards broke even they could take better advantage of their skill than they could in a satellite with less play.

Limit Hold'em Satellites: Winning Principles

4

You've decided that the best way to enter a $1,000 buy-in limit hold'em tournament is to win a one-table satellite to earn your entry fee. Playing a one-table satellite is similar to playing the final table at a larger tournament. Of course, in the one-table satellite everybody begins with the same amount of chips, whereas in a big tournament, not every player begins the final table with the same stack size. However, as soon as you or someone else loses a pot in the one-table satellite and another player builds his chips, the chip counts become lopsided like they are at the beginning of the final table in a big tournament. Chip counts then continue to ebb and flow based on who wins and who loses hands.

Usually in no-limit hold'em satellites you only have to win a relatively small number of pots as opposed to limit hold'em, in which you have to win a series of pots—unless the limits get so high that either you or your opponent only has enough chips to play out one hand.

The Balancing Act

To be a winning satellite player at any game, you must perform a balancing act. The quality of your decisions depends on how well you integrate several critical factors into your game plan. These seven factors should influence your strategy at every stage of the satellite:

1. The strength of your hand;
2. Your position at the table;
3. The playing style of your opponents;
4. The amount of the blinds in relation to your stack;
5. How many opponents you have;
6. How many chips you have;
7. How soon the limits are going to rise.

Table Image

Building an Image

Building an image in a one-table satellite is important because you will be playing against the same players throughout the mini-tournament. Suppose your opponents have been paying attention to your play at the opening levels and have seen you playing very solid poker. Later when you're playing at the third or fourth level with much higher limits, you find yourself short-stacked.

"I'd better try to steal a pot or two," you think, so you bring it in for a raise with a somewhat marginal hand.

"Hmmm, that guy's been playing real tight," your observant opponents think. "I'd better give him some respect. This hand's no good."

He folds. Your solid, conservative image has made it easier for you to pick up some pots when you really need to.

Creating Deception

There are ways of creating deception in the early rounds that will benefit you in the later rounds of the satellite. Especially in the early stages, if your opponents see you playing a rather marginal hand or even if they see you raise from middle position with a hand like Q-J offsuit when you're the first one in the pot, then show the hand down or deliberately expose it, you create an impression in your opponents' minds that you're playing a little bit on the loose side. In reality, you're not. You're just trying to create a false impression that maybe you're a loose goose so that you can capitalize on that image as the satellite progresses.

You get plenty of chips at the start so that if you lose a couple of bets, it really won't hurt you too much. Suppose you come in for a raise with a hand like 8-7 suited. If your opponents see your hand, later on when you have tightened up, that 8-7 will still be stuck in their minds. Based on that impression, they might give you action later when you have pocket aces.

You might have a big hand early on, maybe a big pair, and your opponents will see what you're raising with. Now you may have created another type of false impression in their minds—if that's the only hand they've seen you play in the first round, they may have the idea that you're only going to play when you have premium pairs or big cards. Then you might be able to take a shot at them in a later round with a weaker hand, just because you've created a false impression about the strength of hands that you play. You're capitalizing on your table image.

While your opponents are watching you, you are watching them. If you know that they're studying you, and you think that Ray Reader in seat six has been paying attention and remembers how you play, you can use that to your advantage.

What if they aren't paying attention? If that's the case, working on your image won't do you much good. "Remember the time when I had such-and-such a hand and played it thus-and-thus?" You'd like to point this out to them, but you can't. You want to tell them, "Make sure you don't forget that I did this earlier!" but the words don't come out of your mouth.

Categorizing Your Opponents
Tight Players

Tight players do not usually defend their blinds unless they have a very big hand. They play very few pots.

"They're sitting there waiting for aces or big pairs," according to Brad.

Loose-Aggressive Players

Loose-aggressive players play lots of hands, make a lot of positional raises, and gamble with all sorts of hands including suited connectors and small pairs. They often are the most difficult players to play against because you can't put them on specific hands since they play a wide variety of hands.

"They get very creative," Brad says. "Some people think that these guys just play bad hands all the time, but they don't. They often are very good players, they just play a lot of hands. Sometimes just by putting in a raise, they can read where their opponents are at in a hand. If a tight player calls his raise, for example, the loose-aggressive player knows that he probably has A-K or some other strong hand. Now if the flop comes with low cards, the loose-aggressive player is going to try to take the pot away from him."

If he's a good player, the loose-aggressive player usually will be able to read the tight player much better than the tight player is able to read him.

Weak Players

Weak and inexperienced players make a lot
of mistakes. They call too much and don't get
full value out of their good hands when they play
them. They are not able to read their opponents
correctly. A lot of times weak players will call
raises when they should be folding, such as when
they have marginal hands like K-J offsuit or
K-10 suited against a tight player who has raised
from up front. On other occasions they will allow
themselves to get drawn into a pot by a loose-
aggressive player without any clue as to where
they're at, and either get run off their hands or
call when they are clearly beaten.

They lack a good game plan, primarily because
they are inexperienced in satellite play. If you see
yourself in the weak-inexperienced picture we
have just painted, you are the player we want this
book to help.

Solid-Aggressive Players

Solid-aggressive players are capable of
changing gears based on their chip count and
information they have gathered from observing
their opponents. They may start out playing real
solid and then at about the third level of play
when the limits rise, suddenly they will switch
gears into overdrive. T.J. Cloutier is a classic
example of this type of player—he plays solid,
even a little on the conservative side, during the

early rounds but once the limits rise, he picks just the right spots and plays with you.

Maximizing Your Profits

No matter what your playing style, you can use certain strategies against other types of opponents to maximize your profits in satellites.

If You Are a Tight Player

Developing a tight image can be an asset as the limits rise. You're hoping that your opponents are paying attention. As a smart tight player, you know that you can capitalize on your tight image in selected spots. For example, you realize that you can occasionally pick up a pot with a positional raise, simply because your opponents may believe that it's too risky to call you without a premium hand. But if you play too tight, you simply have to hold a lot of cards in order to win. The better strategy in a short-term satellite situation is to loosen up from time to time, pick your spots, and get creative when the time is right so that you can capitalize on your image.

As a tight player, how can you maximize your profits against a loose-aggressive player? Many times the correct strategy is to simply check-call all the way through when you have a hand that you think might be the best hand. You could have as little as ace-high or you might have second pair. Suppose you're in the pot with A-J and the flop comes Q-J-5 against a loose-aggressive player who's been firing all the way. Your second-pair-with-top-kicker may well be the best hand in this situation, but in case you're wrong, you don't want to jeopardize a lot of extra chips by raising, so the correct play quite often is to simply call him down. He might bluff off a couple of bets, and if you're right, you'll win those extra bets from him with your check-call, whereas if you put in a raise he might muck his hand and you will win only a small pot. With the check-call strategy, you can maximize your win or minimize your loss in case he does have a queen in his hand.

If You Are a Loose-Aggressive Player

If this is your style, you can expect to crash and burn most of the time. However if you don't bust out early and are able to accumulate some chips, you will be hard to beat. The loose-aggressive style of play is the most difficult to defend against and the most unpredictable, thus the hardest for other players to read. In shorthanded play, the loose-aggressive style can be very effective, especially against more conservative players. An avalanche of bets and raises in shorthanded situations often confuses opponents and puts them to the guess. Usually they will guess wrong. When you are the constant aggressor, you opponents will consistently be on the defensive and put to the test. However if your more conservative opponents play back at you, or if they look like they're ready to call you down, you must be able to back off unless you have a strong hand. You need to slow down and sometimes change gears from high to low, from rammer-jammer to solid conservative.

If You Are a Weak or Inexperienced Player

If you are an inexperienced player, you need to get more experience in satellite play if you want to maximize your profits. Learn to read your opponents, realize when someone is playing overly aggressively, pay attention to who is raising in which spots, notice what kinds of hands they're showing down, and identify who will or won't defend their blinds.

Weak players need to learn to call less and raise more. In other words, when you are in a pot, you usually need to be the aggressor, which is a whole lot better than being a calling station. If you just call all the time, you will have to show the hand down, whereas if you are the bettor, you have two chances of winning: The other players might throw their hands away, or you might get called and end up having the best hand. Either way, you win.

If You Are a Solid-Aggressive Player

Most professional poker players are solid-aggressive players. In the long run they are the toughest to beat. They read their opponents well and make good decisions. Solid-aggressive players know when to open up their game and when to put on the brakes. As an aspiring satellite winner, this is the playing style you want to emulate.

To maximize your profits as a solid-aggressive player, you sometimes should put a little more play into your game plan, and become more flexible than the other types of players we have described. As a solid-aggressive player, you have learned to think on your feet, which means that you have the ability to adjust your game in an instant. You can sense both strength and weakness in your opponents and can adjust accordingly. You know when to get the extra bet in, and when to save a bet. You don't play a lot of hands, but you are selectively aggressive when you do.

You know how to capitalize on your strong table image and often will three-bet loose aggressive players with hands that you might fold before the flop against tight players. You run over the tight players, outplay the weak or inexperienced players, and gamble with the best of it against the loose, aggressive players. You are a winner.

Changing Hand Values

You constantly have to be aware of the changing hand values based on the number of players left in the satellite. For example, one hand may be a lot stronger heads-up or shorthanded than it is nine-handed, so you need to learn to loosen up your standards as players go away.

For example, a hand like A-10 usually is not playable from up front in a full game, but it is a raising hand with five or fewer players, even if you are first to act. In general, many of the so-called trouble hands become raising hands shorthanded. Just remember that if you raise and get reraised before the flop with hands such Q-J, K-10, A-9, or small pairs, you should be prepared to put on the brakes if you don't improve your hand on the flop. When an opponent puts in the third bet before the flop, he is representing a lot of strength. It will be very difficult to make him fold any decent hand that he might have started with.

Another point to remember is that there are practically no hands that you should limp with in a shorthanded game. The one time you can make an exception and slow-play a hand is when you have pocket aces. However if you limp with them, your opponents might smell a trap when you just call before the flop. They expect you to raise if you are the first player in the pot, and you usually don't want to disappoint them.

The Chip Count

Since the amount of chips in play in relation to the size of the blinds usually isn't more than ten big bets, chip counts can change dramatically in one-table satellites with the winning or losing of a single pot. Therefore you have to learn how to overcome the chip advantage that another player might have over you after you have lost a hand, and you have to learn to protect the chips that you have, in order to maintain a good chip position.

A lot of times, too, you have to base your decisions on the amount of chips you have versus the amount your chief opponent(s) has. Chip count often will affect whether you play a hand and how much you're willing to commit with it. As you're playing and studying your opponents, you're continually asking yourself "Which players will lay a hand down if I raise the pot?" The answer to that question usually pays off, because it will tell you who is more willing to defend their blinds and who isn't.

"Answering this simple question has paid big dividends for me," Brad points out.

A lot of people make plays in one-table satellites based upon their comparative chip counts. As the satellite progresses and the chips ebb and flow, many times you can actually predict—based solely on the chip counts—who is going to raise the next pot. In six-handed action, for example, if one or two players have passed to the biggest stack at the table, and he's a player who has been raising a lot of pots, you can almost count on seeing him raise with practically anything.

Targeting the Opposition

Weak blind defenders who are playing timidly and can be easily intimidated are prime targets of your raises because you have a better chance of running over them with weaker hands. Obviously big stacks who are willing to gamble with you are not the types of players you want to confront unless you have a solid, premium hand.

"I'd rather play against tight and timid players because not only are they easier to dominate, they are easier to read than loose and aggressive players," Tom says. "If they start firing at you or check-raising, you know that they usually have the goods, whereas you may not be able to put loose and wild players on a specific hand. A lot of loose players crash and burn early, true, but a lot of times they're going to get there with their hands and possibly take you out of action."

If two or three very loose players are at the same table, there's a good possibility that at least one of them will end up with a lot of chips when the others gamble it up against him and crash.

Naturally you would prefer playing at a table that is more balanced, a table with a few weak types, a few super-aggressives, and no solid-aggressive players.

"But if you have a choice between two one-table satellites to play, and one is full of the weak-passive type of player, while the other is filled with rammin'-jammin' gamblers, you are better off in the long run choosing to play against the weak-tights than the rammer-jammers," Tom advises.

Why? Because you have a greater chance of taking control of the table against weak-passive players. You really cannot out-gamble the wild-loose players—all you can do is wait for premium hands and try to pick them off. And what happens if you don't pick up any premium hands?

"You can only play what you get," Brad answers, "and if they're going to be in the pot until the river most of the time, you will have to show down the best hand at the end."

On the other hand, against weak-tight players, you sometimes can bet at the river and win the pot regardless of the strength of your hand. If a weak-tight player comes in with a raise, you usually can put him on some kind of a hand. Suppose you have called his raise and the flop comes with little cards. You've put your weak-passive opponent on an A-K. Sometimes you can take the pot away from him with a weaker hand simply by betting the flop, whereas the looser, more aggressive players will call you down with an A-K in this type of situation. In reality, most satellites have a mixed assortment of player types—some tight, some loose, some solid.

The Effects of Rising Limits

As the limits rise in limit hold'em satellites, each hand becomes more important than the previous hand because the limits usually double at each new level. Satellites are structured for fast play in a limited time frame—usually about five to six fifteen-minute levels. You usually start out with $300 in chips at limits of $15/$30, which means that you start with ten big bets. But after the limits rise to $100/$200, if you haven't gathered any chips and have only what you started with, you'll only have enough to post the small and big blinds twice.

Saving Bets

Suppose the blinds are $50/$100, and you have $500 in chips. On the river you think that you have the best hand. But if you're wrong and your opponent reraises you, you will go broke. In this case you might be better off check-calling rather than value betting to try to pick up an extra bet. That way you'll save the bet, and sometimes you'll be saving two bets if your opponent has you beaten. This strategy will give you an opportunity to come back in the satellite if you lose the hand.

This is a prime example of the difference between playing a satellite and playing a live game. In a live game when you lose an extra bet, it won't materially affect you. But in a satellite where you have a limited amount of chips and a short time to play, saving a bet can affect your results. Losing a single extra bet can make a big difference. That bet you saved enables you to possibly double or triple up on a subsequent hand and maybe go on to win the satellite.

One-Table Limit Hold'em Satellites: Winning Strategies Round-by-Round

5

Although casinos use various structures for one-table satellites, this is the usual setup: After the dealer has high-carded to place the button, you begin play with $300 in chips at a ten-handed table with rounds that last fifteen minutes. The limits start at $15/$30 and progress to $30/$60, $50/$100, $100/$200, $200/$400, $300/$600 until the winner is declared, either by one player winning all the chips or by the remaining players negotiating a deal. The typical one-table satellite is over by the fifth or sixth round, so you can expect it to last for about seventy-five to ninety minutes.

Round One

The limits usually start at $15/$30 with $10/$15 blinds. You would like to increase your stack by 50 percent, which you can do simply by winning one pot, preferably a multiway pot. If you can accomplish this goal, you've done well and are in good position to begin the second level, which is usually $30/$60.

As quickly as possible, you need to learn how to play against each player in each situation. To shorten your learning curve, continually observe your opponents and take mental notes about your answers to the following questions:

1. Who is playing fast?
2. Who is being conservative?
3. Who is playing solid?
4. Who is playing a lot of marginal hands?
5. Who are liberal blind defenders?

You should be playing very solid poker during this first level. Against nine other players you need to play only premium hands such as aces, kings, queens, or A-K in early position. Obviously you'll play these hands from any position, but the main point is that you should not play the trouble hands when you are in the first couple of seats after the big blind. The trouble hands include A-J or lower (suited or unsuited), K-Q, K-J, and K-10 (suited or unsuited). These hands can get you in a lot of trouble up front in a full ring game. If you aren't in the correct position with them and if someone raises or reraises behind you, you almost always are taking the worst of it. You can get involved for a lot of bets, and then be forced to give it up after the flop. Avoid getting in over your head by not playing these hands from a front position.

"It seems to me that more people get in trouble with A-J than with any other hand," Brad observes. "There will be a raise and a reraise, and I'll see somebody come in with A-J. Unless the flop comes J-J-x or they flop a straight, they'll never be able to bet this hand with confidence."

The point is that in a raised pot, the value of A-J goes way down. What we're doing in the first level is playing only premier hands when we're in early position, and waiting for players to bust out or get wounded. As soon as the field thins, you can start playing the players better.

A lot of players set a goal to just get through the first couple of levels. Their reasoning is that two or three players will bust out in the early rounds and, they will still be in action with a much shorter field to conquer, even though their chips haven't increased dramatically. They will have more maneuverability because fewer players are left in action. This also is a viable strategy.

Primarily you're hoping to survive, picking your spots carefully and only gambling early if you're forced to because you're short on chips. You're also hoping that your opponents have noticed that you've been playing solid so that they will give you a little more respect when you come into a pot. When you enter the pot for a raise, your raise will mean more if they perceive you as a solid player.

While you're sitting back waiting for a good

hand to play, you are observing your opponents, figuring out who's gambling, who's playing loose, who's playing tight—and determining the types of hands you might play against particular players. For instance, you might play a somewhat weaker hand against an opponent who has been playing a lot of pots. But against a solid-aggressive player, you might lay down an A-Q, for example, that you may have raised or reraised with against a looser player.

Playing Multiway Pots

Multiway pots are good opportunities to win a lot of chips. The downside is that you also can lose a lot of chips because it is more difficult for a hand to hold up in multiway action. In multiway pots that haven't been raised, what kinds of hands do you want to get involved with?

If you know that there will be four or five-way action and can get in cheaply—even for a single raise—you might gamble a little bit in the hope of winning a big pot. In addition to the premium hands, you might play a marginal hand such as a low pair; middle suited connectors like 8♠ 7♠ or 7♦ 6♦; or unsuited connected cards such as Q♠ J♦, J♣ 10♥, or 10♦ 9♠. You only play these types of hands in late position after two or more players have entered the pot. Also, you cannot call more than a single raise with them. Winning a multiway pot at this point will greatly increase your chances of progressing deep into the satellite. If you are successful in winning the multiway pot, you should put on the brakes and slow down.

Position certainly plays an important role. What if two people limp in front of you and you don't have a big hand? What kind of hand do you want to come in with in this situation? In the first round of the satellite when it's still fairly cheap to get into the pot, you might play suited connectors and small to medium pairs. Follow the two-limper rule that Tom has outlined in his other books: Once two or more people have entered the pot, in addition to the blinds, the pot figures to be a multiway pot even if someone raises behind you. You're getting a fairly good price with two or more limpers (not including the blinds) in the pot, so you can play a variety of hands, trying to win one pot.

You might gamble a little bit in multiway pots to try to win a good-sized pot, and then be very selective about the hands you play from that point on.

"Assuming that I haven't won a pot at this point," Tom explains, "I'm going to play a lot of different hands. Hands like K-Q, K-J, and Q-J—especially if they're suited—go up in value in unraised pots. If it's a raised pot, I don't like any of those hands because they're trouble hands in these situations. I'll slip into the pot with these hands, but I won't raise with them. I won't even raise with an A-J suited or unsuited if there are two or more limpers—I'll just try to see the flop cheaply."

Pairs are good hands to come in with because if you flop a set, you'll have a good hand even in a multiway pot. The general rule is "No set, no bet." If you don't flop a set, you can get away from the hand cheaply. Small and medium pairs should play fairly easily for you if you follow this guideline. If you do flop a set, you're probably going to win the pot about 80 percent of the time.

Suppose you're in a multiway pot with a medium pair, you flop a set, and you must act first on the flop. If you want to build a big pot, lead out and hope that everybody calls. By making this play, you probably will build the pot substantially because chances are, most players who call will stay all the way to the river with any kind of drawing hand. By building a large pot, you face a higher risk of getting drawn out on, but you also create the opportunity to win a lot of chips and thus become a more intimidating force in the second round of play.

Now suppose you make one pair on the flop, and you don't want everyone to stay. How can you eliminate some of your opponents? In this situation, you can try a check-raise. You check what you think is the best hand at the moment, but you suspect that there's a good chance it won't remain the best hand unless you can eliminate players. If you lead into the field, a lot of times they will call-call-call and make a big pot, which will give everybody the right price to try to draw out on you. The best way to prevent them from getting the right price to stay in the hand is to go for the check-raise and hope you can thin the field. Remember that a player often will call a single bet twice, but he won't call a double-bet cold. He can sort of "walk" into a raise by rationalizing that he already has one-half the raised bet in the pot, so it's not much of a stretch to put in the second half. But he might be afraid to rush in for a double-bet in one big increment.

Round Two

The second level of play usually begins with limits of $30/$60 with the blinds at $15/$30. The whole table usually is still in action at the second level, although one or two players may be short on chips, and sometimes one player will have been eliminated. During the second level, however, look for one or two players to drop. Usually no more than two players drop out at this point unless the table is playing very fast. It is from the third level on that players really start dropping.

At the second level you're jockeying for position. You don't want to get too involved in a pot unless you have a strong starting hand. It will cost you more to enter the pot, so from the second level onward you have to be very cautious about entering any pots with speculative hands—as you might have done in the first level because the limits were lower. You're still playing very solid, and you're still getting a feel for how your opponents play—who's tight, who's loose, who's solid, who you can steal from.

If you have only broken even at the first level, you haven't improved your situation, but you're not really in a lot of trouble. You can still play one to two hands, even though you have gone from having ten big bets to having five big bets. Each hand is now much more important. If you did not accumulate any extra chips during the first round, you're going to have to play a hand in the second level. It's possible to sit through two levels without playing a hand and make it to the last five or six players, but if you do, you will have a limited chance of winning because you simply won't have enough chips to play with. Therefore you have to choose a hand to play.

If you're short-chipped when it comes to the second level, you must win some chips. You have to choose some hand, even if it's marginal, and take a stand with it—especially if the limits are going up soon. Hopefully you'll get a good hand to take your stand with, but unfortunately the cards don't usually announce, "Hey, buddy, here're two aces you can take a stand with."

Look for either the best hand—which doesn't necessarily need to be a powerful hand like a big pair—or look for the best situation. You may have to say to yourself, "This looks like the best position for me to take a stand against Player A. He's playing loose and aggressive, and this K-Q just might be the best hand in this situation. I'm gonna take it and run with it, and hopefully I can double up to get some chips."

You usually won't have an opportunity to play a multiway pot in the second level. But if you do get a chance at one, you might be willing to gamble, especially if you have a short stack. You would be less willing to gamble if you have a medium to large stack unless you can get into the pot dirt cheap.

"Dirt cheap means that you can enter the pot for a half of a bet from the small blind," Tom notes, "or for a single bet from late position when four or more people already are in the pot."

If you're short on chips and you're the first one in the pot, you want to come in for a raise. The raise will increase your chances of isolating one opponent so that you can play the pot heads-up. A lot of times in limit satellites, your most likely opponent after you raise will be the big blind. And you will have position on him. It is always important to know whether the big blind is a liberal blind defender or whether he is more likely to fold against a raise. It's always good to know whom you can attack—who will give it up and who won't.

Playing Against a Rammer-Jammer

A lot of times there will be one or two aggressive players who raise constantly. In this case, there's a good chance that your weak ace or K-Q is the best hand, and so you might try reraising them. They have to give you a little respect when you reraise—if they're thinking, they should realize that you've been playing solid through the satellite. But they might not suspect that you've opened up your game somewhat to adjust to the changing game conditions. Some super-aggressive players will bet virtually every time you check to them after the flop. You might not three-bet them, but you can try the check-raise. Or you can let them bet, and if you have a playable hand, though not necessarily a monster hand, you can just call them down. Sometimes these rammer-jammers are drawing dead. But in case they have the best hand, check-calling will minimize your loss. And if you have the best hand, you have extracted every bet possible from them.

Thinning the Field

Say I have an A-K, and the flop comes with an ace. Looking around the table, I see a player sitting in the back end of the pack who looks like he just can't wait to bet. Believing that I can depend on him to bet, I check. Sure enough, he bets. When it gets back to me, I fire in a raise. Now it's two bets to all the players sitting to my left who also checked on the flop. It is highly likely that one or two of them will lay down hands such as second pair, whereas if I hadn't check-raised to make it two bets cold, they might have called the single raise and caught a second pair on the turn to beat me.

You try to thin the field in this situation so that there will be fewer players drawing against you on the turn. The player who made the original bet is almost never going to pass to your check-raise, and you don't expect him to, but you figure that you have him beaten. You simply want to eliminate as many other players as possible to give your hand the best possible chance of holding up with no improvement. This is particularly true when you flop a single pair, in this case a pair of aces with top kicker. If you lead into five or six players and they all call, it seems like someone always hits something that beats you.

Or suppose you lead into an aggressive player and everyone between you and him calls. He raises. Now you have to call the raise, and the chances are good that all the other players will too, because there's so much money in the pot. "Heck, I'm here to the river now," they think. And they actually are making the correct play. What you want to do is make it incorrect for them to call, and that is why you check to begin with. You want the aggressive player to bet so that you can check-raise him, thus making it two bets to the players in between if they want to stay in the pot.

Round Three

You probably will be playing $50/$100 limits at the third level with blinds of $25/$50. The $5 chips usually are taken out of play at this level, though it varies from casino to casino. The average chip count will be $400/$500, so if you have $450, you will be in fair shape. Of course, the average stack of $500 will have only five times the big blind, whereas you started with ten times the big blind in the first level. Usually two or three players are gone by now, and one or two people might be crippled. The limits become even more important in the third round.

Let's say you have held even through rounds one and two, and you begin round three with your original $300 starting stack. You've stolen the blinds here and there or picked up a hand, and you have managed to hold your own. The problem is that with $300 in chips, you have only six times more chips than your big blind. If you go through the blinds three times, you are almost broke—at $75 a round, it costs you $225 to go through the blinds three times. You will need to find a hand soon to change your position and pump up your chips. You can go through the blinds two times, at the most, to try to pick up a hand.

"Personally, I don't want to wait until my second set of blinds come around," Tom says. "After I've gone through them once, my chips are down to $225, and so I am looking for a hand to go with."

How can you maximize your chances of winning a pot? Say that somebody comes in with a raise, and you have A-Q in your hand. You think you might have the best hand. Your opponent has made it $100 to go, and you have only two big bets in your stack. Your best strategy in this scenario might be to three-bet the pot and then lead at it on the flop. The goal of three-betting (reraising) is to isolate your hand against his so that you can play the pot heads-up. Hopefully, your opponent will give it up on the flop. You don't expect him to lay down a premium hand for only one bet on the flop, of course, especially against a short stack.

Suppose your opponent has a pocket pair and you have two overcards to it. Even if he shows you his pocket pair on the flop, you will still have to call him. You're in to the river, committed to looking at all five cards. Why? Because any time that you have more than 50 percent of your chips in the pot, you are committed to going all the way to the river with your hand. If he beats you, that's too bad—but you were doomed anyway because the blinds were going to eat you up if you didn't change your chip position. And sometimes you'll draw out with the worst hand.

By now let's hope you know who you can steal from, who's tight, who has a hand when they come into a pot, and so on. You have to make decisions based on your cards and how your opponents have been playing—and on your chip count and the clock. As people are going broke, your starting hand requirements begin to change because of the size of the blinds and the shorter field. For example, medium-strength hands such as K-10 rise in value in shorter fields.

It's something like playing a football or basketball game in that you're always playing against the clock. Football teams sometimes have to make plays that aren't their standard plays to try to overcome a point deficit before the clock runs out. In the same way, it's very important to keep your eye on the tournament clock so that you'll know when the limits are going up and adjust your game plan accordingly.

Suppose you glance at the clock and notice that the blinds are going to rise before your big blind. You've just been dealt K-10, a hand you wouldn't have considered playing during the first level. But in this situation—the limits are going up, you're going to have to take the blind at the higher level, and you need some chips—that K-10 looks a little stronger to you, doesn't it?

"If I don't play this hand," you think, "the blinds are going to rise in one or two hands, and this may be a lot better hand than I'll get to look at before the limits double." If you come in for a raise in this spot, sometimes everyone will fold quickly, and you might be able to see an extra hand before the limits rise. That is important because when fewer players are left in the satellite, the blinds come around faster.

Round Four

The limits are $100/$200 with $50/$100 blinds. By now four or five players usually have been eliminated. During round four you're probably going to get between eight to thirteen hands, depending on how fast the players are playing and how fast the dealer is getting the cards out. Obviously the fewer the players remaining in the satellite, the more hands the dealer can get out.

"I always encourage people to think a little faster and play as fast as they can," Brad says, "because the more hands we can see, the better it is for everybody."

When it gets to three-handed, you're getting a lot more hands per level. Now in a fifteen-minute round, you might be able to see fifteen to twenty hands because the dealer has to deal so few hands. You're getting a lot more play. The blinds go around a lot quicker three-handed, which speeds up the tournament, which in turn is why satellites only last five to six levels when the rounds are fifteen minutes with $300 in starting chips.

The blinds are a much more important factor in the fourth round because they come around a lot quicker and are quite substantial. They hurt everybody's chip count, even the players with big stacks. It will cost you $150 every round and with five players in the game, you'll have to post the big blind every fifth hand. If you start with $600 in chips and you don't play a hand in four rounds, you are broke! So you can't just sit there—you have to defend your blind and attack other players' blinds as well. The types of hands that you can defend the blind with include any two face cards, any ace, and any pair. The reason these types of hands are stronger now is because you're usually playing four or five-handed, not ten-handed.

In fact, level four becomes a blind-stealing contest. Just winning the blinds will substantially increase your chances of winning the satellite. You have to be very aggressive with every hand you play. And you can expect all the other players to be aggressive too.

Since the blinds are high and come around so quickly, you have to lower your standards for the types of hands you'll raise with. It's usually raise-and-reraise. There is an exception, however: If you want to change your chip position, you might limp in with a big hand, knowing that you're going to get action with it. Aces or kings are the only two hands that you should limp with. Always remember that A-K, which many people think of as big hand, is a drawing hand. You're only going to flop a pair to it about 30 percent of the time. And if you go to the river, you'll make a pair approximately 50 percent of the time. In our opinion, A-K is not a big enough hand to slow-play, and queens are vulnerable to overcards. So that leaves just aces and kings that you might slow-play under certain conditions.

Defending Against a Loose-Aggressive Opponent

By now you have categorized your opponents, so you know how they play and can better judge when and how to defend your blind. Suppose you are holding A-9 in the small or big blind. If a tight player raises, you should think twice before you defend your blind. But if a loose-aggressive player raises, you might take a stand with your A-9. In fact you might say to yourself, "I'm going all the way with this hand," and reraise the aggressive player, even from the small blind.

One advantage of reraising is that it probably will blast any other players—certainly the big blind—out of the pot, so that you have the loose player heads-up. Suppose you have $600 left, he makes it $200 to go, and you reraise it to $300. Now you have half of your chips in, so you are committed to the pot. If he calls, you're going to lead at the pot for $100 on the flop, and then bet your remaining $200 on the turn. Hopefully, he will give it up somewhere along the line. Of course even without hitting the flop, you may have the best hand with an ace-high. "I'm just taking a calculated gamble with this hand in order to change my chip position," you are thinking. You know that you have to improve your position because the blinds are going to rise again very shortly. In this example, you are playing the player, your chip position, and taking into account the fact that the blinds will go up soon.

Defending Against a Weak Player

At the fourth level, there may be one or two inexperienced players left, primarily because they got lucky. Now suppose a weak, inexperienced player raises the pot. Against that type of player, you would have a greater tendency to just call, see the flop, and then make a decision as to how to proceed with the hand. It's harder to know where an inexperienced player is in a hand and whether he is capable of making a laydown. So, you might fire a bet at this player on the flop. Unless he started with a big pair, there's a good chance that he has missed the flop and will fold when you bet.

Whoever aggressively bets at the flop often has the best chance of winning it. So if you haven't fully committed all your chips by reraising before the flop against an inexperienced player, you have the chance to pick up the pot with a bet on the flop or get away from your hand if you think you're beaten.

Sometimes when you fully commit your hand by raising all-in, your opponent will think, "There's no way he could bet that last chip with nothing." You might be able to take the pot away from somebody who has a slightly better hand than yours. For example, your opponent might have an A-10 or A-J and will lay it down because you have been so aggressive and have fully committed with your inferior A-9. This is especially true of inexperienced players because they make more mistakes. Don't forget that in satellites with big increases in limits and short time spans, inexperienced players occasionally win, usually because they got lucky at the right times. The shorter the time and the quicker the blinds go up, the greater the luck factor. Remember T.J. Cloutier's advice: "Any player can wake up with two aces." It doesn't matter whether you are "the best player," you still can't outplay the best hand. Or if you've raised with A-K and somebody calls with A-4 and flops a four to beat you, that's just a part of the game. This is one more reason why professional players grit their teeth so often. All you can ever do in satellites or tournaments is try to put your money in with the best hand and hope that it holds up. You can also take a calculated gamble, hoping that you will win the pot with no showdown. Or you can semi-bluff with a drawing hand and see it get there, so that even though you didn't start with the best hand, you developed it.

Check-Raising in Round Four

If you have enough chips, sometimes you can try a check-raise. Suppose you check and an opponent who is very solid comes in for a raise. If you have a hand of some kind—a pair, an A-K, or an A-Q—you know that you're going all the way with the hand once you have started with it. So you might try a check-raise, if he has enough chips to make him fold his hand. That way you may be able to pick up an extra bet—especially if your solid opponent has seen you playing good poker throughout the satellite. Players respect check-raises at this late stage. If they believe that you're committed to a hand, they need to have a hand themselves in order to continue playing the pot. So sometimes they will lay down a marginal hand, which is what you want them to do.

Say that you come into the pot with a pair of nines, for example. You're committed to your nines, no matter what. Suppose an opponent behind you has two tens or two jacks and raises. You call. "I'm going to bet or check-raise on the flop," you think to yourself. "I'm going with this hand, no matter what, because I'm committed—I've just gotta win this pot." The flop comes with an ace or a king. In order to maximize your chances of winning the pot, you check, knowing that he will bet. He bets and you put in a check-raise. Now you've given him an opportunity to fold the best cards, and if he does, you will win the pot.

Starting Hand Requirements

Knowing that almost every time you enter a pot, you're going to bring it in for a raise—and so is everybody else—what kinds of starting hands do you need in order to raise at this level? Almost any ace-anything is looking a lot better to us now. K-Q is looking good, and all of the trouble hands that we suggested folding in the earlier rounds are much stronger this late in the satellite. If you're the first one to come in, these hands look a lot better. An A-J might even be a reraising hand, whereas when we were going against nine players, we were throwing it away. Now, when we're only going against three or four players, the chances of A-J being the best hand are a lot better. We also know that everybody else usually has opened up their requirements and are capable of raising with a lot less strength. So at level four, you might be reraising with the same A-J that you threw away in level one. The same goes for all the other trouble hands—they rise in value as the number of players decreases.

Do I Call or Do I Raise?

What kinds of hands do you need in order to call a raise? Generally speaking, especially in tournament poker, you always need a stronger hand to call a raise with than you do to raise with.

"If I'm not in the blind," Tom advises, "I might try to three-bet the pot to drive out the blinds when I have a hand that I think I might play to the river. I may even three-bet with the pair of nines in Brad's previous example. Say that I am on the button and someone raises in front of me. I would reraise with nines to make sure that I drive out the blinds."

In a situation like this, being able to correctly read your opponents pays off. Making the right decisions about when to fold, call, raise, or reraise hinges on your skill and diligence in observing how your opponents' play.

Round Five

The limits are $200/$400 with $100/$200 blinds. It's getting close to the end of the satellite. Although they occasionally go the sixth level, most one-table satellites end at the fifth level, either by playing it out or by the remaining players striking some sort of deal. Certainly it should end by the sixth level at the most.

By the fifth round, you're usually down to

between two and four players, depending on how tight the table is playing. There usually is one big stack and one little stack, with a player or two in between. Or there might be one big stack and two short stacks. The chip distribution often will determine whether you want to play the satellite through, or go to Monty Hall's solution, "Let's Make a Deal."

The higher the blinds become, the more similar limit hold'em play becomes to no-limit play. This is true because, just like in no-limit hold'em, it becomes so easy to get all-in that almost everybody is in jeopardy of going broke, with the possible except of the big stack at the table. In fact, the blinds are so high that it's almost like flipping a coin, particularly if the two remaining players are equal in ability. Even if one player has a skill edge, if he loses one hand at such high limits—and anybody can lose a hand—he's in trouble. Therefore it usually is in the best interest of both players, including the so-called better players, to make some sort of a deal or save.

Playing Against Short-Chipped Opponents

You need to be very aware of the stack sizes of all your opponents. It is critical that you know how likely a player, especially a short stack, will be to shove in the last of his chips. You don't want to double up the short stacks by playing marginal hands. For example, 10-9 suited sometimes is a playable hand, but you don't want to raise a short stack all-in with this type of hand when you think he is committed to his hand. All you have is 10-high, so if he has a hand with even a single face card in it, he is the favorite heads-up. And he's going to have to call you. Suppose he has only $400 or $500 with the blinds at $100/$200. If he's the big blind, he already has $200 in the pot with just $300 left in his stack. Even if he has a weak hand, he's almost forced to call you if you raise. Therefore if you have a marginal hand, you don't want to play it in this situation.

Now suppose you have something like K-9 or K-5. You are in the $100 small blind and your opponent is in the $200 big blind with $300 left. If you raise it to $400 you are sure that the big blind is going to call. So to maximize your chances of winning it, you just call by putting in the extra $100. Then no matter what comes on the flop, you bet. You're giving him the opportunity to throw his hand away. Essentially, you are delaying a bet in order to maximize your chances of winning the pot. He is likely to miss the flop—you both are—but by betting into him on the flop, unless he hits something, he has to fold his hand in order to save his last $300 in chips.

If you had raised him before the flop, he would have had to call the raise. In that case, you would both see all five cards, and that would give him more of a chance to beat you. By just calling before the flop from the small blind, you might still have a good chance to pick up the pot, even with a hand as weak as 9-2. It really doesn't matter what you have; delaying a bet until the flop will help your chances of winning the pot against the short-stacked big blind.

Playing Shorthanded

When you get shorthanded with only two or three players left, you have to be very aggressive. It will hurt you too much to have to put up the blinds at this point, so your attitude is "I'm gonna close my eyes and here we go! It's time to gamble!" If you have three times the big blind, you have to go with a hand before the blinds get to you. We'll go into more detail on shorthanded play later in this book, but here are a few pointers that you can use in the fifth round.

With a very short stack, you simply cannot afford to take the blinds. You have to double up to put yourself in a competitive position. However, if you have a hopeless hand such as 7-2 or 8-3 and you know that you're going to get called, you're better off waiting and taking the random blind hand.

But when you're short-stacked and playing heads-up, if you have something as good as marginal suited connectors (J-8 or J-7, for example) or any unconnected hand that is better than jack-high, you're going to fire in your chips to try to double up. If somebody calls you, hopefully his random cards are lower than yours. If not, you might get lucky and draw out. By being aggressive, you give yourself a better chance to come back, especially from a short-chip position.

Even a hand as bad as Q-4 is playable. Suppose you raise with Q-4 and your opponent calls you with a hand like 9-7. Heads-up, your queen-high is a favorite over his 9-7, even though the 9-7 may play better in a ten-handed game.

Some players become more conservative with a short stack and just try to hang on, but they tend to squander chips when they have a big stack by playing too many marginal hands. But in satellite play, the shorter your stack and the later it is in the satellite, the more risks you have to take. Otherwise your position will become eroded. Don't forget that on-land satellites usually are winner-take-all unless a deal is made. If you get heads-up and someone has a 5 to 1 chip advantage over you, you're in no position to make a deal based on chip count, but you should still be open to offers. So you simply have to make a move designed to improve your chip position. Usually by the sixth round (if the satellite goes that long), you're almost always heads-up.

The Art of Deal-Making in One-Table Satellites

Deal-making in satellites is like any other verbal business proposition in that any player can make an offer for a settlement. Sometimes the proposition will be fair to everyone, and sometimes it won't. Usually a player will offer a deal that is in his own favor, of course. After hearing the proposition, the other players can either accept the deal, make a counter offer, or decline any deal whatsoever.

If the prize pool is divided among the two or sometimes three finalists with no money left over to play for, the satellite ends as soon as the deal is made. But if the deal involves a "save," it continues until one player wins all the chips. A save is an amount of prize money that players agree to keep for themselves. After agreeing to a save, the players compete for the remaining money in the prize pool.

Suppose there are only four players left and you want to calculate the value of your chips so that you can estimate your equity in a potential deal negotiation. You're playing for a $2,000 tournament seat that cost you $200 to enter, plus the vig. You started with $800 in tournament chips, four times the amount of the buy-in, which is the standard ratio of chips to buy-in at many casinos. Ten players started in the satellite, so the total number of chips in play is $8,000.

In a land-based tournament, if you would like to actually "see" your equity in the prize pool, divide your chips in half once and then divide them in half a second time. For example, suppose you have $1,600 in chips. You split your stack into two equal stacks of $800 each. Then you split one of them again so that you now have three stacks in front of you. The value of the smallest stack is your cash equity in the prize pool. In this example, your worth is $400 cash, plus your share of the cash back that usually goes along with the seat. If you are playing on-line, you can mentally divide your chip total by four to come up with the monetary value of your chips—in this example, $1,600 divided by four equals $400.

Now suppose you're playing heads-up and your opponent has suggested making a deal. You have $2,000 in front of you, so you know you have $500 cash value in the settlement ($2,000 divided by 4), the equivalent of one satellite chip plus your share of the $100 cash back.

In a lot of satellite deals, players will agree to save a chip or save a buy-in. Or when it gets to heads-up play, each player might take one chip if their stacks are fairly even, and then play for the third chip. For example, if my opponent and I each have about $3,000 in chips in a satellite for a $1,500 tournament seat, we might agree to each take a $500 chip and play for the remaining $500 chip. Certainly it's okay to simply lock up a monetary win. Though you may not win the satellite, you've made money in it.

As Tom so often says, "You never go broke taking a profit."

Sometimes you're so low on chips, you can't hope to make any kind of a deal. Since you're gambling nothing to win the thing, a lot of times you will just open up and fire in your chips.

"You have only one way to go, and that's up," Brad states. Hopefully you will get lucky and double up a couple of times so that you will have a shot at winning. The two times that you are least likely to make a deal are when you're very short-chipped and when you have a big chip lead. All of the in-between situations require the most skill in deal-making.

Of course, nothing says that you ever have to make a deal in a satellite. It all depends on your skills, your chip count, and the nature of your opponent. If you have the lead and you think your skills are about equal to those of your opponent, you might offer him a reduced settlement—it never hurts to ask. Or if you're trailing in the chip count, you may very well ask for a deal in which you get a premium for your chips, particularly if you think that you are the more skilled player. Sometimes you can even trade a piece of yourself in the main tournament or accept a piece of your opponent. Trading pieces works best when you know that your opponent is a successful big buy-in tournament player. I know of several people who have traded ten percent of themselves in a satellite for the satellite seat and gone on to cash big in the main event. Hans "Tuna" Lund once won $14,000 in this type of deal. He saved 10 percent with his heads-up opponent, then went on to cash in the main tournament for $140,000. This type of save works particularly well when it's heads-up and the only way that either of you can play the tournament is by winning the satellite seat. Just be sure that your opponent is capable of winning the tournament. You also can refund your opponent his satellite buy-in plus 10 percent or more of your potential tournament win, if you think that's what it will take to tie up the seat.

If you're playing heads-up with someone who is super-aggressive and the blinds are very high, you probably are better off making a deal. Why? Because ability doesn't count for much in a situation where someone is shoving his chips in on every hand so that you can never tell where he's at in a hand. This type of player is capable of shutting you out. He's forcing you to pick up a hand and flip a coin with him. It gets to the point where it all has to go in the middle, even in satellites, especially when you already have committed a big part of your chips. Here is Doyle Brunson's take on playing against this type of player heads-up for all the marbles:

"There were two of us left in a hold'em

tournament at Binion's and the other guy couldn't play at all, he was really a bad player. I had about a 2 to 1 chip lead over him and we made a deal. 'Doyle, why did you make a deal?' a friend asked. It was simple: While my opponent couldn't play a lick, he was raising $50,000 or more on every hand. One time when I made a stand, he threw his hand away with a 7-2—and he'd raised me $80,000 with it! Well, I mean that kind of guy is capable of beating you! Suppose he wins two or three hands, or I'm not holding any cards and just keep letting him run over me—I don't have a big enough ego that I think I can't be beaten. So I made a deal with him based on our chips."

Brad tells the following story about a deal he was glad to make:

"I once was playing three-handed in a $500 buy-in satellite for a $5,000 seat in the championship event at Harrah's, Las Vegas. When we started play with only three players, I was very short on chips, having just a little bit more than I started with. The second player was in the same situation. The third player had almost all the chips. The chip leader said, 'You want to save $500 each?' but I didn't hear it exactly right. I thought he said, 'Do you want to take $500 for your chips?' There was no way in the world I was going to take $500—I was ready to gamble three-handed. But when he repeated it the second time, I heard him correctly. He was offering me and the other short-stacked player an equal save of $500, even though he was way ahead in chip count. So I'd be able to continue playing with all my chips and still be guaranteed to make my buy-in back if I lost. I quickly said, 'Okay!' So did the second player. The chip leader just wanted to save his satellite buy-in, I guess. He then went on to easily win the satellite, but because of his generosity, I got my buy-in back anyway."

How Do You Know When It's Time to Negotiate a Settlement?

It's crunch time—time to make a deal. The crunch comes when the blinds are so high that you have to put in about 25 percent of your chips for the big blind. For example, suppose you're three-handed with $6,000 chips in play. The three of you are about equal in chips with $2,000 apiece. The blinds are $200/$400. You say to yourself, "Hey, it's deal time!" because you can't even call a raise without totally committing yourself to the pot. Everybody is pot-logged in this case.

There are several ways in which you can strike a deal at crunch time. You can cut up the prize pool by chip count, or you can negotiate it by having each player save a chip. Or save the buy-in. You can always make a suggestion. People can say yes or no, or they can bounce the idea around and come up with a new mix. Sometimes players don't realize that it's possible to make a deal in a satellite, so throwing out an idea may open them up to this possibility.

Another factor in making a deal when it's shorthanded is who is in the big blind. For example," says Brad, "if three of us are left, we're all about even in chips and I have the button, I'm going to wait one hand before I suggest a deal because I don't have any money in the pot. 'Let's play one more hand,' I'll say if someone suggests making a deal at that point. I want to let the forced blinds play their hands. That way, I might pick up a hand on the button and be able to win the whole enchilada. With $2,000 chips each and the blinds at $200/$400, for example, one of my opponents has 20 percent of his total chips in the pot and the other has 10 percent in it. I have a free shot at going after the $600 in the pot, and even if all I win are the blinds, I've changed the whole situation, and put myself in the chip lead. Now suppose I'm the big blind, the blinds are $300/$600 and we each have $2,000 in chips. 'Hey, you guys wanna chop this thing up now?' I'll ask. These techniques work in limit and no-limit satellites alike."

No-Limit Hold'em Satellites: Winning Principles

6

Tex Sheahan once said that playing no-limit hold'em is like walking a tightrope across a river of sharks. Or as one player put it, "I don't like no-limit because I can play perfect all day and then make one mistake and get busted." On the following pages you will find our opinions on how to handle many of the finer points of no-limit poker. For starters, we suggest that you review the list of strategic factors in tournament play that we gave you in Chapter Four, as they apply to no-limit as well.

The Balancing Act

To be a winning satellite player at any game, you must perform a balancing act. The quality of your decisions depends on how well you integrate several critical factors into your game plan. These seven factors should influence your strategy at every stage of the satellite:

1. The strength of your hand;
2. Your position at the table;
3. The playing style of your opponents;
4. The amount of the blinds in relation to your stack;
5. How many opponents you have;
6. How many chips you have; and
7. How soon the limits are going to rise.

These seven factors interrelate in satellite play. In some situations, your chip count will play a more important role in making a quality decision than the strength of your hand. In other scenarios, your table position and the playing style of your opponent(s) will take precedence over your chip count. Here are a few examples that illustrate how you can balance these factors when deciding how to maximize your profits or minimize your potential losses.

Scenario One

You are one of three players left in the satellite. You and your two opponents have $1,000 each in satellite chips, so you're dead even. The blinds are $100/$200. The button throws his cards in the muck. It's your turn to act from the small blind, and you look down at two jacks.

The big blind is a very aggressive player, and you know that the blinds are going to rise to $200/

$400 in five minutes. How do you play the hand?

You limp if you think that the big blind will come over the top of you for a raise. That way, you can get all your chips in before the flop.

Now suppose everything in this scenario is the same, except that the big blind is a conservative player. How do you play your pocket jacks in this situation?

You make a small raise to between $400 and $600. You are forcing the big blind to put in more chips if he wants to see the flop. You don't want to give a conservative player a free flop. You know that he probably will just check if you limp. But if you raise, he might think that you're trying to steal, and he may call the raise. With your pocket jacks, you want to get the money in before the flop.

Scenario Two

You are one of three players left in the satellite. With $3,000 total satellite chips in play, the button has $1,500, you have $750 in the small blind, and the big blind also has $750. The blinds are $100/$200.

The button is a conservative player and throws his cards in the muck. The big blind is a very aggressive player. Again you look down at two jacks. How do you play the hand?

You move all in. You believe that the aggressive big blind will think that you're trying to steal the pot and will call your all-in raise with a variety of marginal hands. If you limp (just call for an addition $100), you will be giving him a chance to see a free flop and perhaps outdraw you with a weak hand.

Now, suppose the big blind is a solid player. How do you play your pocket jacks?

You still raise. The point is that whether the big blind is solid, aggressive, or even passive, your strategy doesn't change whatsoever. Your chip count is the important factor in Scenario Two. Two jacks is a good hand, so you want to make your opponents pay to try to draw out on you.

Scenario Three

You are one of three players left in the satellite. With $3,000 total chips in play, you have $1,500 sitting on the button. An aggressive player is sitting in the small blind with $750. A solid player is sitting to his left in the big blind, and he also has $750. Your hand is K-10 offsuit.

The blinds are $50/$100. How do you play the hand?

Your K-10 figures to be an above average hand in this scenario, but it isn't a hand that you want to put in a lot of chips with. If you raise and one of your opponents comes over the top of you, you probably will have the worst of it. You don't want to take the chance of trading chip positions with either of them. With the blinds at $50/$100, there aren't really enough chips in the pot to warrant jeopardizing your chip lead with a hand such as K-10 or Q-J. You might do one of two things:

1. Limp for $100, and then fold if either opponent raises; or
2. Fold the hand to begin with.

Now suppose the situation is the same except for one factor: The blinds are $100/$200. How do you play the hand?

You move in. In this scenario your K-10 is looking better. With higher blinds coming around so fast and $300 already in the pot, the players in the blinds are more likely to play substandard hands weaker than your K-10. You want to pick up the pot, so if you play the hand, you play for all your chips. With hands such as Q-J, A-8, or a small pair, your play is the same.

Let's change the scenario one more time. This time you have K-10 on the button with $1,500 in chips sitting in front of you. Both your opponents in the blinds are wild men and they each have $750 in chips. How do you play the hand?

It depends on the size of the blinds. If the blinds are $100/$200, you move in. If the blinds are $50/$100, you have two options:

1. You can raise and be prepared to call if one of the blinds reraises; or
2. You can opt to not play the hand at all and simply fold. With two super aggressive players in the blinds, the chances are good that if you pass, one of the blinds will move in on the other one. Sometimes you suspect that two people are going to go to war against each other. If you think that may happen, why not just get out of their way when you have a marginal hand such as K-10, Q-J, A-9, or a small pair?

Now suppose you have pocket aces. What's your play? You have two options:

1. Limp in, hoping that one of your blind opponents will come over the top and give you some play; or
2. Raise a small amount in the hope of enticing them into the pot.

What if you have two jacks? In that case you definitely move all in. You don't want to limp and take the risk of running into an overcard on the flop—you'd hate to see the big blind win it with something like a Q-3 offsuit. Also, your opponents may think that you're trying to steal when you move in, and therefore, they may call you with weak hands.

Now suppose the small blind is a solid player and the big blind is an aggressive player. How would you play all the hands we have discussed in this scenario? You would play them the same way, even if they both are solid players.

But suppose the blinds are $50/$100 instead of $100/$200, and both blinds are tight players. You are dealt K-10 on the button. What do you do?

You raise $300, the standard amount. If one of them moves in for the rest of his chips, you know that he has a much better hand, and so you fold. The difference in how you play the hand this time is the nature of your opponents. When one of them is aggressive, you play the hand more solid because the aggressor is likely to come after you. When they both are tight, you can raise with the K-10 because there's a good chance that you can pick up the pot right there. If one of them raises, you know you're beaten because they are tight players who usually would only raise with a premium hand.

Scenario Four

Five players are left in the satellite with $3,000 total chips in play. The blinds are $25/$50. You have $600 in chips, which is the average amount of chips. You are sitting under the gun and look down at K-J suited or unsuited. On your immediate right, you see that the big blind has the lead with $800 in chips. How do you play the hand?

With the blinds at $25/$50, you just limp into the pot if you want to play because the big blind has you out-chipped.

But suppose the big blind is short-stacked with only $200 in chips. In this scenario, you bring it in for $200 with your K-J, which is an above-average hand when you're playing five-handed. By raising $200, there's a good chance that you will be able to isolate against the big blind and play him heads-up. Further, your raise puts the big blind to the test: If he calls you and loses the hand, he will be out of the satellite.

Let's change the situation again by reversing the chip counts. Suppose you have $200 in first position, and the big blind has $600. You will have to take the big blind on the next hand. How do you play the hand?

You move all in with your K-J. You don't care whether the big blind or anyone else has $600, $800, or any other amount. You're going to take a chance with the hand to try to pick up some chips and improve your chip position. In this scenario, your chip count in comparison to the big blind's chip count is the determining factor in how you play the hand. Even with a worse hand, such as K-9, you might move in under the gun with your $200 in chips, whereas if you had a lot chips, you wouldn't even consider playing the hand.

Now, suppose you're on the button with K-J. In this case, you automatically raise all-in with your $200 in chips.

But suppose you're on the button with a lot of chips, the small blind also has a lot of chips, and the big blind has only $200 in chips. In this scenario, you don't want to jeopardize a lot of your chips so you raise to $200, just enough to put the big blind all in.

What if you're on the button and the big blind, who is a tight player, has $600 in chips? In this case you might consider raising to try to steal the pot from him. If he is a loose-aggressive player, you might raise a little bit if you have plenty of chips because even if he calls or comes over the top of you, the chances are good that your K-J is still the best hand. Or you might just limp. Now your loose-aggressive opponent in the big blind may think to himself, "Why did he just limp? Maybe he's trying to trap me, slow-playing a big hand." Your deceptive limp may actually slow him down.

Now, suppose the small blind is short-stacked with only $200 in chips and the big blind has plenty of chips. You are on the button with K-J and have plenty of chips. What do you do?

You raise. If the small blind has a marginal hand, he may think to himself, "If the button is trying to steal, this is a good chance for me to double up. His raise probably will blow the big blind out of this hand and I'll be getting a good price for my hand." This is a good spot for the small blind to call because he knows there's a good chance that he will get to play the hand heads-up with you.

In this scenario, most of the factors that you must balance to make good decisions in no-limit hold'em are coming into play—your position, the number of chips you and your opponents have, whether they're aggressive or solid, the size of the blinds, and the number of players at the table. You always have to balance the importance of one factor against the importance of the others in reaching a decision.

Game Discussion

No-limit hold'em is a game that requires judgment. You may decide to play a hand one way and then, after discussing it with a friend who is knowledgeable, find that he would have played it differently. Who is right? Neither of you is necessarily dead right or dead wrong. It all depends on how you and your friend balanced the way your opponents were playing, the amount of chips they had, how many chips you had, and the value of your hand in that particular situation.

The right way to play a hand is not set in stone—there is more than one way to play every hand. Understanding that, debate with other good players on the topic of how to play specific hands in certain situations can make you a better player. If you remain open-minded enough to see both sides of the story, you can grow. Usually your differences of opinion occur because you and your poker buddies emphasize different factors.

Now let's take a look at some of the winning principles for playing no-limit hold'em satellites.

You Need a Stronger Hand in Order To Call Than You Do To Bet

When you are the first player in the pot and come in for a raise, you put your opponents to the test. If they are smart, they realize that they need a stronger hand in order to call your bet than you need in order to bet. Conversely, if an opponent moves in on you, you must have a hand in order to justify calling. Although he doesn't need to have a hand to raise, you need to have a hand to call his raise.

When somebody moves in, decide how strong you think his hand might be. If you think that your opponent is out of line, you sometimes might call with a somewhat weaker hand. Suppose you have an A-10, for example. You might consider calling if you think the raiser is just trying to put a move on you. He may be going all in, for instance, because he wants to try to improve his chip position by blowing you out of the pot.

When you are short on chips, you are more likely to take a risk by raising with a hand such as middle suited connectors—but only when you are the first one in the pot and can make a big enough raise to, hopefully, get your opponents to lay down their hands. This is why we say that when you are first to act, you can raise with a weaker hand than you can call with. As the first bettor in the pot, you put your opponent(s) to the test—but when an opponent is the first one in the pot, he puts you to the test.

You Don't Need to Win a Lot of Pots in No-Limit Hold'em

In limit hold'em you have to win a series of hands to be successful, but in no-limit you only have to win certain key hands. The pots you win in no-limit play are sometimes much bigger than they are in limit games because either your whole stack or your opponent's whole stack is involved. When the money goes in, you want to have the best hand. In no-limit when you have to put in all your chips with only a drawing hand, it's usually too expensive.

Sometimes you might semi-bluff at the pot with a drawing hand if you're just trying to pick up the pot and you think that a bet will win it. If you get caught, at least you have some outs. Suppose two or three people come into the pot, and you pick up the nut flush draw on the flop. "If I raise this pot a pretty good amount," you think, "I have two chances to win—either they will all throw their hands away, or I might hit the flush and win the pot if they call." The other result is that you get called and lose the pot because you don't make the hand.

How Much to Bet

A lot of people who are accustomed to playing limit hold'em are now experimenting with no-limit hold'em, and most do not choose the appropriate amount of chips to bet when they first start playing no-limit poker. They either under-bet or over-bet the pot. Many of them simply make a mini-raise, that is, double the amount of the big blind—the amount they are accustomed to raising in limit hold'em. Inexperienced players who make mini-raises don't realize that they could just limp instead. There is hardly any difference between raising to two bets and just putting in one bet in no-limit hold'em. And some novices have just one move—all-in. We would like to give you a better idea of how much you should bet in no-limit hold'em so that when you raise, you will be confident that your betting strategy is correct.

We like to bring it in for between three and four times the size of the big blind when we are the first one in the pot. But a lot of players make the mistake of gauging the size of their raise by the strength of their hand. In *Championship No-Limit & Pot-Limit Hold'em*, T.J. Cloutier and Tom McEvoy suggest that you always raise the same amount—three to four times the big blind—so that you won't give your opponents any clues about the strength of your cards.

"With limpers already in the pot," Tom adds, "I increase my opening bet about one unit for each limper, maybe slightly more. For example if the blinds are $25/$50 and there are two limpers, I would make it around $300 to go. If I am short-stacked with a couple of limpers, I don't mind going all-in before the flop, even if it means that I have over-bet the pot. For example, suppose I have only $500 left, and there are two limpers in the pot. Instead of making it $300 to go, I will simply move all-in. I would also move all-in against short-stacked limpers even if it meant slightly over-betting the pot. The reason I do this is because I want to win it right there, or at least make them fully commit.

Is there a benefit to making just a mini-raise? Someone who just raises double the size of the big blind usually is inexperienced in no-limit play—he's playing a no-limit satellite like we would play a limit hold'em satellite. Or he might be a very sophisticated no-limit player like 2000 World Champion Chris Ferguson, who sometimes makes this type of bet. People put in a mini-raise for one of three reasons:

1. To create some deception as to the strength of their hand;
2. Because they may have a speculative hand such as J-10 suited; or
3. Because they are inexperienced.

Your challenge is to figure it out.

"If people have become accustomed to seeing a sophisticated player put in a double-raise," Brad says, "later on in the satellite when he has two aces and really wants action, he might put in a mini-raise to lure an aggressive opponent into coming over the top of him. His mini-raise is deceptive because his opponents never know where he's at in the hand. Usually however, players who just put in a double-the-blind raise will have a hand such as Q-J suited or a small pair, and they just want to look at the flop."

Players tend to follow the leader. That is, if the first player who raises in the satellite over-bets the pot by bringing it in for $100 when the blinds are $10/$15, everyone who raises after that often follows suit by raising the same amount.

"When that happens," Brad notes, "I usually ask out loud 'What's the minimum you can come in for?' I ask that question because if my opponents start raising too much, they stop me from being able to limp in and thus force me to have a big hand to be able to play with them."

There are certain situations, however, where you can over-bet the pot by a little bit. For example, suppose you get lucky in the first round and one of your opponents throws off all his chips to you. Now you have chips, and you need to protect them. You don't want to give anybody a shot at making two pair when you're holding pocket aces for a small amount of money, so you might over-bet the pot a little bit, knowing that it is very hard to give aces up in a satellite. Sometimes it works to your advantage in another way, too. One of your opponents might think, "He's betting too much, he's just trying to steal this pot." And he calls you when he shouldn't.

Reopening the Betting with a Mini-Raise Can Cause Trouble

One of the biggest mistakes inexperienced players make in no-limit hold'em is reopening the betting by making a mini-raise. Two people limp in, it goes around to someone who is inexperienced, and he doubles the bet (raises the size of the big blind). This situation happens so often—limp, limp, limp, and somebody doubles it. "Hey, you wanna raise it some more?" is just what he's asking for.

"When I'm in the big blind and this happens, I want to reach over and smack him," says Brad. "He's opening it up for the limpers to reraise — a lot! One of them might even have limped with pocket aces. I know that if I get the right flop, I can bust somebody who has two aces. But now I might not even call, knowing that one of them might reraise and shut me out."

Essentially the mini-raise has simply reopened the betting. When several aggressive players are at the table, one of them is liable to interpret the mini-raise as weakness and reraise with almost anything. "Oh, yummy," they think, "I'm gonna pick up this pot!" If this is the case, you have to be more careful about the hands you call a mini-raise with from the big blind, especially when people have limped in.

What do you think people are trying to accomplish when they make a mini-raise? They aren't going to drive their opponents out of the pot, especially not the limpers. They are simply going to reopen the betting, which could be detrimental to their chip health. Or they may believe that their mini-raise will build a good pot. But there is no reason to try to build a pot in no-limit hold'em because people will gamble anyway — there could be just one chip in the pot, and you can still move in for all your chips. People will gamble more in no-limit than they will in limit. They will put in their money after the flop, even if the size of the pot is relatively small. The two main reasons for raising are:

1. To win the pot when everyone folds; or
2. To make other players pay to try to draw out on you when you believe you have the best hand.

When You Raise All-In, Do It with a Specific Goal in Mind

Over the past few years, it seems that players have started moving in all their chips more frequently. When a player moves all-in, it often means that he is inexperienced or doesn't know how to bet. Of course there is a benefit to moving all-in, namely that no one can outplay you after the flop because if someone calls, the decision is over with, and you cannot make a mistake. You may have made a mistake by shoving all-in to begin with, but you cannot make any further mistakes since you are going to the river. No matter what cards come on the flop, even if you did make a mistake in betting, you could get lucky and draw out on your opponent.

The all-in move seems to be more prevalent in low-limit satellites. Some people refer to it as the "one-bet mentality," because the only bet that some players seem to have is the all-or-nothing bet. We don't want our readers to think that the all-in bet is the best way to go—there is a time to go all-in, and there is a time not to.

For example, moving all-in can be an effective tactic when you believe that you're outclassed in the satellite. Maybe you're playing against a world-class player—even champions play satellites—and you think you're at a skill disadvantage. In this case, even a top player cannot outplay you after the flop when you're all in, whereas he may be able to outplay you from the flop onward if you still have chips to play with.

One advantage to moving all-in rather than betting, say, half your chips, is that other players cannot possibly think, "If I reraise him, he will throw his hand away." You're already all-in, so they know you are going all the way.

The biggest disadvantage to going all-in is that if you get called—unless you have over-bet the pot with a big pair—you're almost always going to have the worst starting hand. You're just gambling that no one has a better hand than yours. "I'm going all-in," you think, "and if you've got me, that's okay. If you don't, you'd better throw your hand away."

There is another situation in which you might consider going all-in. Brad explains it this way:

"It seems that players today have a tendency to think that when you bet a certain amount of chips, you'll throw your hand away if they can come over the top of you. For this reason I have changed my play a little bit to adjust to this mentality. There are times when I will move all-in simply because I want them to know that I am committed to the pot and will not lay down my hand. In the past when I had $500 or $600 in chips and I bet half of them, anybody who knew me would understand that when half of my chips were already in the pot, I would never throw my hand away. They understood that I didn't care if they came over the top of me, I wasn't going to run away from those chips. But since many players today don't understand this concept, I've changed my play by going all-in just so they'll know that I will not lay the hand down."

"At the 2003 World Series of Poker, we were down to eight players out of a starting field of 531 in the $1,500 no-limit hold'em tournament. I raised about half of my chips with an A-Q. Everybody folded around to Amir Vahedi, who thought about it at length and then moved all-in on me. Being certain that I had the best hand, I called him instantly with the rest of my chips. We turned over our cards and sure enough, he only had an A-J, making me a big favorite in the hand. I was sick when a jack came on the flop and I caught no help on the turn or river. Amir went on to win the tournament.

"In retrospect I believe that if I had moved in to start with, he could not have called and undoubtedly would have thrown his hand away.

But because I had raised only a half of my chips, he didn't understand that I was committed and probably thought that I would fold if he came over the top of me. If I had gone all-in, I would have left Amir with only two options: call or fold."

Many inexperienced players do not understand when their opponents are fully committed to the pot. They do not know that you absolutely are going to put in the rest of your chips, and their lack of knowledge can allow them to put a bad beat on the better hand. You make this all-in play with a medium to short stack so that your opponents know you're going the distance with the hand. Or if you have a very big stack against a short stack, you do it so that the short stack knows that he has to fully commit in order to call. Although you would be more likely to make this play from the fourth round onward when the blinds are hefty, you could actually make it during any stage of the satellite, depending on your chip position.

You Can Get Free Information from Your Opponents— and Give Some Back

You need to stay tuned in every minute, watching the other players and noting the hands they expose or turn up at the showdown. You can also get free information from them.

"Sometimes a player will raise the pot when I'm in the big blind and everyone throws their hand away to me," Brad notes. "I'm the only player left to challenge the raiser, and I look down to find 10-4 offsuit. Knowing that I'm going to fold, I might say, 'Look at this, you've caught me a little weak with only a 10-high. I'll bet you can probably beat that.' And I muck the hand. 'Yeah, I can beat it,' the raiser might answer. 'Look at this' and he shows me his hand. Now I have some free information on what he's raising with."

This type of information will give you some help in reading your opponents and a better idea of the kinds of hands to play when someone comes in for a raise. In some situations, you can give free and deceptive information to your opponents.

"Suppose I'm bluffing—I've made a positional raise with a marginal hand—and an opponent reraises me," Tom adds. "I might say, 'You've caught me with my hand in the cookie jar' and show him my 10-8 as I fold."

You only show him your hand if you think it will throw him off his game. Of course you don't intend to bluff him again—next time you will have a hand.

"But if I do intend to bluff him a second time after I've gotten away with the first bluff," Tom says, "I won't show him my hand. It just depends on the image that I want to create in my opponents' minds."

If you bluff a player and then show your cards after he folds, you know he's probably going to come after you the next time. You would be more likely to show a bluff to the type of player who is likely to get his nose open and start steaming.

In one-table satellites you play with the same players throughout the satellite, so people usually will remember it when you do things like this. As a general rule, however, it's better not to show anything unless you think it might be to your benefit and will have a positive result. For example, you may have a strong hand against a very aggressive player, come over the top of him, and show your cards when he folds. You want him to think that you don't reraise unless you have a strong hand because the next time you reraise him, you might not have as strong a hand. Usually when you raise or reraise and then show your hand, you should show only your good cards—if you show them at all—because you want to maintain a good, solid table image so that you will get respect. This works well later when you want to steal a pot.

Maintaining a solid image is important because when the blinds go up, during the third and fourth levels in particular, you are going to have to pick up more blinds. And if your opponents think that you only raise with strong hands, you will have a greater chance of success. In the first and second rounds, you're setting the stage. You want them to think, "When he come in for a raise, beware of him!" When you need to pick up the blinds in later rounds, it's important for people to look at you and think, "That guy's real solid. He doesn't come in unless he has a hand." But remember that it can work against you too. If your opponents think you're too tight, they might not give you any action when you do have a hand.

Your Style of Play Affects Your Chances of Winning

In no-limit poker, excessively tight play doesn't cut it. It will, however, allow you to survive longer. But suppose you get to the final three or four players and they all have you out-chipped three or four to one, so you're forced to play a marginal hand—what have you accomplished? In other words, very tight play usually doesn't allow you to win satellites because you just don't get enough hands, or you don't get enough action on your good hands. You have to use a different style of play to be most effective in satellites and tournaments.

Solid-aggressive is the style that we recommend. You don't want to play a whole lot of hands, but when you do play a hand you want to be aggressive, unless you're trying to trap by just limping in during the early rounds. At the second level the blinds go up but they're still low, so you might do some limping with hands that you would raise with in the next round when the blinds have doubled. You still don't want to take any big risks during the second level because there isn't enough blind money to justify it. But from the third level on, that begins to change.

You Can Play Small Pairs and Connectors in Select Situations

Because of the potential future bets you can win, there are bigger implied odds in no-limit hold'em than there are in limit hold'em. This leads to the question, "When do you play the small pairs and middle connectors?"

"I like limping in with small to medium pairs because if you flop a set, you have a strong hand, one you might win a lot of chips with," Brad notes. "Obviously you would rather play them when your opponents are playing rather passively. With a pocket pair, you can even call a raise that doesn't hurt you much and try to flop a set if you feel sure that you will get paid off if you hit the flop. Just remember that you can't take much heat with them, certainly not heat that jeopardizes too many of your chips."

Suppose two or three people have limped

into the pot ahead of you. You have something like 8♥ 7♥ and just limp as well. Limping shows weakness on most of the players' part, therefore an aggressive player in later position might take advantage of this situation by raising. His reasoning is that if his raise knocks out the blinds and the first limper, he will pick up the pot uncontested. In other words, in this situation it looks like free money.

If you limp in from anywhere up front, be forewarned that a lot of times, you're just setting yourself up as a target because to some players, you show weakness when you limp from a front position—and they're going to come after you. When you limp and an aggressive player takes it away from you, remember that he might try the same thing again when you're holding A-A or K-K.

On the other hand, always beware of limpers. It is a good idea while you are following the action to make a mental note when a player limps. Ask yourself, "What would Fred limp with at this level?" And always count the amount of chips he has in front of him.

Sometimes you can call with a hand that is even weaker than connectors or small pairs. For example, suppose you're in the little blind and two or three people limp in. You have 10-5. It only costs you one-half a bet to call. Should you?

"Usually I'm going to call that half-bet," Brad

says, "because unlike in limit hold'em where I can only win a few bets, in no-limit if I catch the right flop I might be able to win all of somebody's chips."

You'd love to see the flop come 10-10-5, of course, but even if it comes 10-5-2 you're happy, especially if an opponent has limped in with K-10 or A-10, because you can win a big pot with your two pair. Even though 10-5 is a garbage hand, its value goes up because the implied odds are so big in no-limit if you catch the right flop.

Now suppose you are in the big blind with an inferior hand such as 8-7 offsuit. Someone has raised a double-bet and two or three players have called. You might also call from the big blind, since all you have to call is one more single bet and you have the right implied odds.

Slow-Playing Can Be a Lethal Weapon

Should you ever slow-play a big hand in a no-limit hold'em satellite? Yes, if you think that someone will raise if you just limp into the pot. Or you can slow-play by checking on the flop when you feel certain that an aggressive player will bet. Sometimes you might even check both the flop and the turn when you have the best hand, because you realize that some aggressive players cannot restrain themselves from betting when you check to them twice.

The idea is to get as much money as possible into the pot, which you expect to win. Sometimes slow-playing is the only way to do that because if you bet, you are pretty sure that your opponents will fold their hands. Your check on the flop may allow them to catch up and possibly give you some action on your premium hand.

You Can Delay Stealing the Pot Until After the Flop

Suppose you are one in front of the button with a K-10, and no one has entered the pot. The blinds are $25/$50. The button has an equal or bigger stack than you do, and the big blind has $50 in the pot with $75 in chips left in his stack. You know that the big blind is going to play almost any hand because he already has almost half his chips in the pot. In this situation you can use the delayed steal strategy.

Here's how it plays out: You flat-call before the flop. Your unorthodox limp into the pot often will freeze the bigger stack on the button from making any type of play. Why? Players are accustomed to seeing everybody bring in the pot for a raise. Now a big stack—in this case, you—suddenly limps, thus raising the suspicion that he might be slow-playing a premium hand. For this reason the button may fold a hand that he otherwise may have called with because he is fearful that you are laying a trap.

Assuming that the button folds, you and the big blind will be heads-up. Because you haven't put him all-in before the flop, the big blind doesn't have the chance to routinely see the hand through to the river and possibly outdraw you. You now have the opportunity to bet if he checks to you, whether or not you have flopped anything. When you bet, he will have a hard time calling you if he has no pair. He probably will opt to wait and take the small blind on the next hand.

It wouldn't be terrible, either, for you to bring it in for $125 to $150 to put the big blind all in. Whether you limp or raise, if the big stack on the button makes any type of serious reraise, don't worry about whether he's bluffing. Simply throw your hand away.

In making this type of play, you have risked the minimum. If you run into a real hand behind you, you can get away from your hand cheaply. You also have created confusion in your opponents' minds. Further, if the button raises behind you after you've limped in, and you subsequently fold, you have done some useful advertising. Your opponents might think: "When this guy limps, it doesn't mean anything." Then, later on when you limp with pocket aces, someone with that thought stuck in his mind might raise it. Your limp has set the stage for a later play.

Now, suppose you have a medium stack about par for the course, and you virtually never limp. If you are the first one in the pot, you'll bring it in for a raise about three to four times the size of the big blind. Play solid poker, but play aggressively when you come into a pot.

When you are short-stacked, you might consider just moving in with any hand you want to play. Put in your chips and take your chances.

Look for Opportunities to Come Over the Top of an Opponent

When the blinds are coming up fast and you know that you need to make a decision, or when the limits are about to increase, look for a situation where you can go over the top of an opponent. Sometimes when the blinds are fast approaching, you might take a stand just before the limits increase to try to avoid having to put in the increased blind money.

Keeping track of the clock and how much time is left in the round is important. Although it is less important during the first two rounds, from the third round onward the clock increases in importance. While the blinds are at $25/$50, you want to keep track of how soon they will be rising to $50/$100. The fourth and fifth rounds have the biggest jumps in the blinds, from $50/$100 to $100/$200. This is the stage when the satellite usually is played out to its conclusion.

Knowing that the blinds are going up sometimes will affect your play. For example, say that you have a K-10 in first position. If the blinds are going up on the next hand, you'll be more willing to play that K-10 than you would be if you knew that you could look at a few more hands before the blinds rise, especially if you short-stacked. Why? Because the K-10 figures to be better than the random blind hand you will be dealt on the next deal. If you have a hand such as 9-8 suited, that's a different story. You would be concerned that if you get called, you almost certainly will be going uphill with the hand. If you are short-stacked with the 9-8, it is almost certain that someone will call you.

You might also take a look at the players in the blinds to determine whether they might lay down a hand. What is the strongest hand they will throw away? Always remember that it takes a better hand to call with than it does to raise with. So, based on your opponents' chip counts and playing tendencies, you have to evaluate how likely they are to fold a hand.

"Sometimes I will take a shot with a marginal hand," Tom explains, "just because I think that the big blind won't defend."

If you're short on chips, the big blind is the player who is most likely to call you because he already has a substantial investment in the pot.

Before you move in with a short stack, always ask yourself, "How much will my chips hurt my opponent's chips?" In other words, will you be putting him in a bad position if he calls and loses the hand? A player who has a medium stack may not get broke if he calls a short stack's raise and loses, but he can be severely damaged. For that reason, he'll often think twice before he plays the hand for a raise.

Play the Button Like a Fine Violin

Some people think that when a raise comes from the player on the button, the button always has a weak hand. If an opponent thinks you're trying to steal with a weak hand, he is likely to reraise you. You need to recognize which players have that mentality so that you can use it to your advantage. For example, when you catch pocket aces or another high pair on the button, you can raise knowing that your opponent probably is going to reraise. His reraise then allows you to get maximum value from your good hand.

Now suppose you are on the button and you

slow-play your hand. When you just call, the blinds are likely to suspect that you have a big hand and are trying to trap them.

"Occasionally I will limp in on the button with hands like J-9 suited just to see the flop cheaply," Tom says. "I don't think the blinds will come over the top because they're afraid that I have a bigger hand than I actually have. Then if an ace comes on the flop and they check to me, I can easily pick up the pot. But if they bet into me, I fold."

In this situation, if the blind checks when an ace comes on the flop, it's almost guaranteed that he doesn't have one, but he suspects that you probably do. You don't have to risk much when you bet, just a small bet will get the job done.

Don't Despair When You Get Behind

If someone has two or three times your chips, all you have to do is go all-in with him on one hand and you'll double up. Then you will be even with or have more chips than your opponent. When a player has exactly a 3 to 1 advantage over you in chips, you're only two hands away from breaking him. You have to look at your whole stack as though it's one bet. That's why you don't push the panic button if you get out-chipped by the opposition.

In no-limit satellites it isn't unusual to see two or three players get busted out in the early rounds. The better the player you are, the better you're able to adjust to the shifting circumstances. Even with a smaller stack, stronger players adjust and play a better shorthanded game than the opposition.

"When I won the World Series in 1991," Brad relates, "I was heads-up at the championship table with Don Holt, who had about $2 million to my approximate $200,000. At that point all I was doing was looking for hands to double through with, and then double through again.

"Fortunately for me I was able to double through to approximately $400,000, then to $800,000, and then to $1.6 million. Then on the last hand, I held the K♠ J♠ and flopped a pair of jacks for the win. So, don't give up when you are behind, just look for hands that you can double up with. Pretend that you are chopping down a tree with an axe—one chunk at a time—until it falls down."

One-Table
No-Limit Hold'em
Satellites:
Winning Strategy
Round-by-Round
and
Player-by-Player

7

The structure of a typical one-table no-limit hold'em satellite has players starting with $500 in chips. The blinds are usually $10/$15 in the first level of play. They rise to $10/$25 in the second round, and go up to $25/$50 in the third round. After the third round, the blinds begin to double on each round. The blinds rise to $50/$100 in the fourth round, $100/$200 in the fifth round, and so on through the rest of the satellite.

In this chapter we begin by discussing general principles of play for each round. We follow that discussion with specific pointers on how to adjust your play according to the number of players at the table.

Round One

The relative strength of a starting hand depends on the number of players in the game. Because more people are playing against you when the game is ten-handed, you need a stronger starting hand than you would need when the game is five-handed, for example. A marginal hand that you would throw away when the game is ten-handed may become playable when the table is short. Also remember that when the game is ten-handed in the early stage of the satellite, there isn't much blind money in the pot to fight for, therefore you have less reason to try to steal pots with substandard hands.

Even though blinds are small early in no-limit hold'em satellites, you can still get broke on the first hand you play—as opposed to limit hold'em satellites, where you are protected by bet limits. In no-limit, you can move in your whole stack at any time, no matter how small the blinds are. A lot of times you'll see two or three players go out during the first level of play, which virtually never happens in limit hold'em satellites.

"I like it when two or three players get busted in the first round," Brad remarks. "Even if I don't get their chips, it's to my benefit to have them gone because then I don't need to have as big a hand to play a pot since the field has been thinned out."

Position

Your position at the table is especially important in no-limit hold'em. Play more conservatively in early positions. In the first three positions after the blind, you definitely want to play only premium hands and usually bring it in for a raise when you enter the pot. You can play more liberally from middle to late position in unraised pots when two or three limpers are in the pot. You are looking for a situation where you can win a pot and maybe double up, while trying to avoid getting eliminated. Always remember that you can't win the satellite during the first round of play, but you can lose it if you make a mistake.

In the first level when the blinds are low, you might limp in when you are in position in order to possibly do some advertising. Say that you're sitting in a middle position and you pick up a hand like 7♣ 6♣ or a little pair. You limp in with the hand and everybody notices that you've just limped. An aggressive player sitting behind in late position fires in a substantial raise. You can't play the hand in this situation, so you fold.

You hate losing the money, but you hope that your advertising will pay dividends later on. Your opponents become accustomed to seeing you limp in when the blinds are very low, that is cheap advertising. Then when the blinds rise in the later rounds and you limp in with a big hand like pocket aces or kings, they probably will think nothing of it. In fact when the blinds are big, having pocket aces or kings would be the only reason to limp in when you're the first one in the pot, in which case you're hoping someone will come over the top of you.

In the early rounds you've been advertising by limping in, hoping to see a flop, and you've set a false image in your opponents' minds of how you really play.

Trouble Hands

Trouble hands can be even more trouble in no-limit hold'em than they are in limit hold'em. The blinds are very small in relation to the risks involved, so why get involved with a K-Q when someone raises in front of you? You could lose your whole stack with this trouble hand.

Slow-Playing Hands

In no-limit hold'em, expect to see more players slow-play their hands, trying to trap you. This happens because in no-limit hold'em, you can wipe out your opponent's whole stack in one pop—as opposed to limit hold'em, where you can only make one extra bet by slow-playing.

All-In Mentality

Also look for the all-in mentality in some of your opponents, especially inexperienced players who do not know how to bet their hands. If they have a hand they want to play, they often will over-bet the pot by shoving in all their chips simply because they don't know the correct amount to bet. They are either afraid to play a pot or they don't know what else to do. Say it's the first level with $10/$15 blinds, and you have a hand that you want to raise with. If you are the first one in the pot, the normal raise would be $45 to $60, three to four times the big blind. A big raise would be $100, or about seven times the big blind. This is a good indicator of inexperience. When someone moves all-in or makes huge over-bets in the first round, you can probably assume he is an inexperienced player.

Adjusting Your Strategy for Ten- or Nine-Handed Play

When we say that we're going to play a pot, we usually mean that we're coming in for a raise if we are the first one in the pot. During the first level, however, you might occasionally limp.

"I'm trying to look at flops during the first round," Brad says, "because I think that players make a lot of mistakes after the flop. I don't need to have aces or kings to look at the flop. If I can see the flop for the right price, I can play lots of hands. But if I am forced to put in a lot of chips before the flop, I need to have a premium hand. In no-limit hold'em, if I play something like 8-7 and flop two pair or a straight, I can break somebody with the hand, thereby getting maximum value from my initial limp."

You can figure that if you double up in the first round, you will have enough chips to last through five players. That is, your chips will be on par with the average amount of chips when there are only five players left in the satellite.

"I want to hold on to my chips so that I will be there when we get to shorthanded play," Brad says. "I'm looking for people to get out of line. I prefer playing little pots, but if any major money goes into the middle, I want to be the one putting it in. I don't mind losing a little pot, but when the big chunk goes in, I want the boss hand so that I have leverage."

You want to be sure that you're one of the survivors when the satellite gets to the fourth round and that you have at least average chips or better. To do that, you have to protect your stack.

What kinds of hands do you raise with in the first round? If you're in early position, you want to have a big pair, A-K, or possibly A-Q to bring it in for a raise. Be somewhat leery of raising with A-J—there's always the chance that someone behind you will reraise, and you can't take a lot of heat with A-J. You might want to just limp with A-J, but if you do raise with it, we suggest that you raise only three times the size of the big blind ($45 in the first round of play).

With A-K or A-Q, we also suggest raising three to four times the big blind. Then if one or two players call, you can take a stab at the pot on the flop to try to pick it up, whether you hit or not. If you hit the flop, you might check it and give someone behind you the opportunity to bet so that you can check-raise him. The check-raise is very strong in no-limit because you can win all of your opponent's chips at one time. So if you get a hand to trap them with, you can open the noose with a check and then tighten it with a check-raise when they bet.

We know that raising from up front with hands such as A-10, K-J, or K-Q is shaky, but what about raising from middle to late position with these hands? Even if nobody is in the pot, you still do not raise with these trouble hands. Why? Because the blinds are so small that there's practically nothing in the pot to steal. And if you get played with by somebody who reraises behind you, he probably has a better hand than you. You should only consider raising with one of these marginal hands if:

1. A player with very few chips has limped into the pot in front of you; and
2. The blinds are players who will give up their hands easily.

In any other circumstances, you need a premium hand in order to raise from middle to late position during the first round of play.

"In the first round I don't do a lot of raising," Brad says, "because with $10/$15 blinds there is only $25 in the pot."

When you see someone limping in no-limit, especially if he's sitting in the first few seats, a warning light should flash in your mind. A limper can be dangerous. They can always be limping with a big hand. So you might just limp with the trouble hands if you want to play. Of course you don't really need to play them because the blinds are so low in the first level. You want a premium hand when you raise because there's nothing to pick up anyway. The ratio of reward to risk favors the risk when the blinds are small.

"I'm just trying to manage the size of the pot," Brad says, "and I'm protecting my chips. I don't want to lose any chips because they're valuable."

Your chips are your army and the fewer soldiers you have, the more valuable each one is.

Round Two

In the second level, the blinds usually go up to $10/$25. Things will be pretty much the same as the first level. You're seeing who's playing fast, who's tight, who's scared. You're also looking for people that you might be able to steal a pot from later on—as well as identifying players who might try to steal from you. Knowing these things, you can decide whom to play with when somebody comes in for a raise and can better judge what kinds of hands you want to play. You have to perform the balancing act.

Adjusting Your Strategy for Eight- or Seven-Handed Play

Hand values begin to change somewhat when seven or eight players are left. That is, the trouble hands gain some value. Usually you're in the second round, but sometimes the third round, when the game gets to seven-handed play. If you are under the gun when it's seven-handed, you have only three players behind you to the button. From seven-handed on, you hardly ever limp when you are the first one in the pot. Either come in for a raise or throw your hand away, unless you are purposely limping in order to disguise a big hand and hoping that someone will raise behind you.

Round Three

At the third level, the blinds rise to $25/$50, so it costs $75 per round to play. Usually six or seven players are left, unless the table is playing very tight The normal raise is $150 to $200. Now you have to pick up a few more pots because the blinds are coming around faster. If you already have a lot of chips, your goal is to preserve your chip position. If you're trailing, your goal is to gain on the chip leaders or at least survive and maintain your relative chip position.

Players now are playing more aggressively to pick up the blinds. Even the tighter players have to start opening up their game because of the larger blinds and the smaller field. Excessively tight play won't get the chips in no-limit hold'em because it's hard to get that many good hands. And once a tight player does get a premium hand, if he gets played with someone else may have a better hand. You have to start capitalizing on your table image to pick up some pots.

Adjusting Your Strategy for Six-Handed Play

When the game becomes six-handed, chip count and position begin to play a more important role in your decisions. The types of hands that you might play from early position include A-10, K-Q, K-J, and medium pairs, and you'll probably bring it in the pot for a raise. However, if you have a lot of chips—for example, you have tripled up—you may be reluctant to get involved with these hands from first or second position. This is an example of how your chip count affects your play. If you are medium to short-stacked, you are more willing to take some risks and play more aggressively with these trouble hands. You might even want to gamble from a late position with a hand such as 10-9 suited.

Now suppose you have the chip lead—you've built your chips up to around $1400. With that size stack, you can zero in on the shortest stacks. You play your table position strongly. You can play hands such as pocket tens or jacks aggressively. You virtually never limp into a pot unless you're on the button or one spot in front of it and at least one limper already is in the pot.

If you have doubled up or tripled up, it is very important to protect your chips. You already have enough chips to play the satellite down to three players. You don't want to start playing hands such as J-10, 10-9, or 9-8 suited from a front position. A lot of people play these hands, but they are big-time chip burners. You want to guarantee yourself the best chance of making it to the three-handed fight, at which point you can be much more creative in your playing strategy.

"If you do nothing except maintain the chips you have," Tom explains, "you will be on par with the number of chips you need to play three-handed."

When you have the lead or a lot of chips, you don't want to play a hand for a large amount of money unless you're pretty sure that you have the boss hand. Furthermore, you would prefer to play against one of the shorter stacks so that you won't risk getting broke or crippled if you lose the hand. You want to attack players who have short stacks because they can't come over the top of you for very many chips. If a short stack catches you with a weak hand, he cannot substantially damage your stack.

However you must be aware of players who

are so short-stacked that they are forced to call a raise with almost any hand. You don't want to double them up, so avoid semi-bluffing them with marginal starting hands such as middle connectors—although you might play a small pair. Remember that if you have a 10-9 suited and your short-stacked opponent has a Q-2 in the big blind, he is the favorite heads-up. You need to know when it is better to call than to raise. Sometimes it's better to just call and try to pick up the pot after the flop.

Round Four

"I think the fourth round is the most critical round in the satellite," Tom says, "because the satellite is up for grabs at this point, so you have to make the most critical decisions."

In the fourth round, the blinds are $50/$100, and from here onward, it is very important to know when your chips are in jeopardy, when you are committed, and when you need to change your position by gathering some chips. You must constantly perform the balancing act.

Suppose you start the fourth round with $700 in chips. You're sitting in the $100 big blind and somebody raises to $300. If you call the raise, you will have $400 left. Now you have several options. If the raiser is a player who has been stealing a lot of pots, you can come over the top of him for all your chips with a decent hand such, A-Q, A-J, or better. If he is someone that you think is out of line quite often, you might even try going over the top of him with a very weak hand if you think that he will give you lots of respect and might fold. You are transferring the pressure right back to him, especially if he knows that you've been playing solid. At the least, he has to pause to think. If you were playing limit hold'em, he probably would call you. But in no-limit hold'em where he has to put in so many more chips to call, he will be put to the test. While he's hesitating, you're thinking, "Oh boy, now I have a chance at winning that $300 he raised me."

In the fourth level, you're not really looking for a strong hand like you would be if you were playing limit hold'em. At this point in a no-limit satellite, you're looking for a hand to come over the top of somebody with. You are working through the level and gathering chips all the way without showing down many, if any, hands. Almost all the hands during the fourth round are played before the flop—it's raise and take it, or raise-reraise and take it without seeing very many flops. Or it might be raise-move-in-call, and the play is over before the flop.

Stealing the blinds at this level becomes very important, and you're always trying to figure out who's out of line when they try to steal your blind. You are reading your opponents and trying to figure out what they actually have. If you are fairly certain that you have the best hand and you think they're weak, you can try to make them lay down a hand by coming over the top of them before the flop. You're not looking to see flops, you want to win it before that. In fact when you come over the top of someone, or raise trying to steal the blinds, remember that you are making a play in the hope of improving your chip position. If you get broke in one of these plays—say, you run into a better hand or get drawn out on—that is just a part of the game. In order to play no-limit hold'em well, you must make these plays when the time is right.

Limping in Round Four

We said earlier that you can limp with the little hands. If your opponents have seen you do this in earlier rounds, you might try limping from up front with a big hand during the fourth round. You're hoping that somebody will raise behind you so that you can come over the top of him. Or if you limp with a somewhat lesser hand and your opponents don't raise because they respect you and think you might be limping with aces, it's easy to pick up the pot with just a minimum bet on the flop.

"If I'm in the small blind against the big blind," Tom adds, "I may flat-call with a strong hand in the hope that the big blind will come over the top of me. Then I can either reraise or flat-call and see the flop. Either way, I usually am the favorite. In other words, if you have a big hand in the small blind with John Bonetti, who is well-known as an aggressive tournament player, sitting in the big blind, you aren't going to raise—you're going to flat-call hoping that he will hang himself."

Part of the reasoning behind this type of play is that a lot of players cannot stand to be checked to twice. Therefore even if they don't raise before the flop, you can check to them on the flop if you catch something good. You're showing weakness, and a lot of aggressive players who can't stand the thought of just checking will bet. You're giving them the opportunity to stick their chips into the pot so that you can get them. You're giving them a chance to bluff, to make a mistake.

You know who the aggressive players are by now, so you know who's going to bet when you check to them. You also know who probably is going to throw away his hand if you raise him.

In no-limit hold'em, it is extremely important to know how to play before the flop. The importance of this skill changes as the limits rise. In the earlier limits, you will be looking at a few more flops but from the third and fourth rounds onward, you're playing more and more to win the blinds. Blind stealing and identifying who is out of line when they try to steal your blinds is very important at this level. When you think someone is out of line, you have to have the heart to come over the top of him. As Mike Sexton once said, "Sometimes it's hard to pull the trigger more than once." But sometimes you have to pull it in order to give yourself a chance to win. "You have to be willing to die in order to live," is the way that Dr. Max Stern put it in *Championship Stud.* And it's always nice when you wake up with two aces and are able to snap off somebody who is out of line when he raises in front of you.

In other words you're not going to win a satellite unless you're willing to take some risks—and the biggest risk is the move-in bet. When you are the first aggressor in the pot, you put your opponents to the test. If they are smart, they know that you know that they need a stronger hand to call you with than you need to raise them with. And when an opponent moves in on you, you must have a hand in order to call him. He doesn't need to have a hand to raise, but you must have a hand to call the raise.

When somebody moves in, you always have to decide how strong you think his hand is.

"Sometimes I'll call with a somewhat inferior hand if I think my opponent is way out of line," Brad advises.

If you look down at a weak ace, for example, you might consider calling if you think that the raiser is trying to put a move on you. Is he raising because he's in trouble? In particular, is he short on chips and needs to improve his chip position? Sometimes, as you follow the play around the table, you will know that if everyone passes to Action Jackson, he will raise.

Playing Your Opponents' Stacks

From the fourth round onward, you are playing the size of your opponent's stack very strongly. It is very important to know exactly how many chips your opponents have because their stack size affects how you play against them. For example, you might over-bet a pot, knowing that you're putting the decision to your opponent—if he calls and loses, he will go broke. Or you might bet an amount that makes it appear as though you are committing all your chips when, in fact, you may not be intending to fully commit. You're just trying to put some pressure on your opponent. For example, if he has $600 in chips and you bet $250 or $300, he may lay the hand down if he believes that you are committed to the pot, when you actually could be trying to steal from him.

Adjusting Your Strategy for Five-Handed Play

When you get to five-handed play, you're probably in the fourth round with the blinds at $50/$100. Average chip position is around $1,000. Normally, nobody limps at this stage of play. The typical raise is about $300 to $400, three to four times the big blind. If you have $1,000 in chips and raise to $300, you can escape from your hand—if you think it's the right thing to do—and still have a reasonable stack of $700 in chips. However the next time you come into a pot, you would raise for all your chips.

Now, suppose you have $600 in chips. If you raise to $300 you will make it easier for someone to call and have the chance of outdrawing you on the flop. So instead of raising to $300, you raise all-in before the flop—now your opponents know there is no way they can take you off the hand.

Let's say that you have a stack of $1,000— average for your table—and a solid player brings it in for a raise from an early position. How strong a hand do you need in order to call him? Remember, you need a stronger hand in order to call a raise than you would to raise the pot yourself. Hands such as A-10, K-J, Q-10 suited—hands that you might have considered playing if you were the first one in the pot—go down in value if the pot has been raised, and you simply toss them in the muck. Even an A-J is questionable as a calling hand in this situation, and A-Q is marginal, meaning you'll just have to use your best judgment as to whether to play. You might play if you have a pocket pair that is tens or better, but it depends. If you're a little short-stacked yourself, you might even take a stand with nines, eights, or sevens. In other words, the shorter you are, the more likely you are to take a stand with medium pairs.

"There is one exception, however," Tom notes. "If the solid player is one or two hands away from the big blind and is short-stacked, I may play with him. If he has average or above average chips, I don't want to get involved."

Part of your decision always depends on the clock. How soon will the blinds rise? If you know the blinds will rise in a couple of minutes, an A-Q and medium pairs will look much stronger to you than they did during the first round.

Now suppose the blinds have just risen. In this case, you might decide to wait if a good player raises under the gun. You know that he usually has a good hand and isn't pushing the clock because the blinds are already high, so you back off.

A lot of times when your chip count is average or lower, you don't have much maneuverability. When the table is five-handed, the blinds come around pretty fast, so you sometimes will have to play relatively weaker hands. If you know that the blinds are going up in a few minutes, for example, you need to accumulate chips to give yourself a good chance of survival at the next level. The shorter your chip count, the more risk you have to take in order to improve your chip position. The higher your chip count, the more likely you are to protect your stack. You must continually perform the balancing act.

Adjusting Your Strategy for Four-Handed Play

Things really speed up with four players left. The blinds usually are at the $100/$200 level, and two of the four players are always in them. The average stack is $1,250. This means that if you start the round with an average stack and you bring in the pot for the average raise of three times the big blind ($600), you will have half your chips in the pot. And when this happens, you almost always will be committed to the pot.

"If someone raises behind you, you're in a damned-if-you-do, damned-if-you-don't situation," Tom comments. "If you fold, you will be very short-stacked in relation to the blinds. If you call, you at least will be giving yourself a chance to win, even if you are taking a little bit the worst of it. In cases like this, even if I don't like the situation, I will not abandon my children, so to speak."

In other words, you're better off risking the pot in order to improve your chances of winning the satellite. If you win the pot and double up, you've either busted or crippled your opponent, further improving your chip position. In fact, you will have almost 50 percent of the chips on the table if you win the pot in this scenario.

When someone raises in front of you, you can call with a middle pair or better, including any big ace. At a four-handed table, anyone who raises most likely has a less than premium hand, unless he is a super-conservative player. Suppose the chip leader raises and you have a small pair, such as sixes, or a weak ace, such as A-9, and you will have to go all-in if you want to call him. In this scenario, you might decide to wait for a better situation. Of course if you have a strong ace — A-K, for example — you probably will call his raise.

"I'm just not a strong enough player to lay down an A-K," Tom admits, "unless someone bets and another player raises in front of me."

An A-K will be close to even money against any hand except a pair of aces or kings. You need to improve your chip position in order to win the satellite, and you have a hand that usually will give you an almost 50 percent chance of winning the pot. Sometimes one player will be in a dominant position and the other three players will be hanging on with shorter stacks. If you are one of the shorter stacks in this scenario, be willing to gamble more with marginal hands. One of the shorter stacks usually will be more timid than the others — he's the one you want to attack if possible, especially if he is very short-chipped. Keep in mind, however, which players are most likely to feel committed to the pot. They are the ones you do not want to attack with a marginal hand because they are more likely to call.

Round Five

As a general rule the satellite ends during the fifth round, although it occasionally will last until the sixth round if a couple of players are ultraconservative. Sometimes it doesn't even get as far as the fifth round; it might end in the fourth round if one player wins it all—which is rare—or the players agree to a settlement. In no-limit hold'em it often is more difficult to make a deal because one hand can dramatically change things. If an opponent has two-thirds of the chips and you have the other third, you will reverse positions with him if you double through him once. So you often play for it rather than make a deal.

Assuming that $5,000 is in play and three players are left, the average stack will be around $1,700, and the blinds will be $100/$200. This means that if you make or call a normal raise, about half of your chips will be in play before the flop. A lot of players do not realize when they are in trouble with their chip count. When they get down to the wire, they tend to hit their panic buttons. How many times the amount of the big blind do you need to have to be safe? If you can only get through the blinds twice, you're in bad shape, but you still have a chance to survive.

Remember that when you're playing three-handed, the big blind comes around every three hands. If you can only post the big blind twice, you will need to take a stand fairly quickly. If you have enough chips to make it through the blinds three times, you're in pretty good shape.

"I think you need enough blowout power to pick up the blinds without being contested," Brad comments. "I believe that if I have three or four times the big blind, which is the normal raise, I will have a chance to pick up the pot without a contest."

If at all possible, you don't want to let your chips get so low that it would be correct for your opponents to call any bet that you make. If you only have double the size of the big blind, your opponents usually will call you with all sorts of marginal hands—and they usually are correct in doing so.

"My panic problem sets in when I have less than four times the big blind," Brad adds. "So, I usually will play some sort of hand that will give me a chance to pick up the blinds so that I won't fall below that. Even if I'm in early position, I'll play a weaker hand, trying to keep my chip count from falling below four or five times the big blind. If I can do that, I know I'll have a chance of winning a pot uncontested. Then it'll be just a move-it-all-in shot, hoping I can pick up the pot before the flop. If I get called and I don't have the best hand, I might get lucky on the flop and draw out on my opponent. And what happens if I draw out? I change my chip position."

Sometimes you just have to get lucky.

"If you can make a big enough raise that they will lay it down," Tom says, "you're better off putting it all in with literally nothing than waiting for the big blind to take its bite out of you."

In other words, when you get so short that you can't go through the blinds, you only have one chance to win: You will have to show down the best hand. We're trying to help you avoid that option by showing you how to give yourself a chance to win without the best hand.

If you are down to two or three times the size of the big blind and you have a truly hopeless hand like a 7-2 or 8-3, what do you do? If it is highly likely that your opponent will call you, you're better off waiting for the big blind.

Calling an All-In Bet

Now suppose that it's three-handed, and you're in the big blind with chips—you're in first or second place, say. Fred is the short stack, and he desperately needs chips. He goes all-in for $400, double your big blind. What do you do?

You call him in a heartbeat with any ace, any pair, any two cards 10 or higher, any king-small—indeed you can call him with any reasonable two cards if you have the lead and his all-in bet is no more than double the big blind. Why? Because you have a chance to take him out of action. What if he only has $300 and goes all in? You can call him with any two cards; you call him in the dark.

"One major weakness I sometimes see in otherwise good players is that they will throw their hand away in this type of situation," Brad comments. "You're never that big a dog."

So why do they fold when they shouldn't? Usually it's because they're afraid of doubling up their short-stacked opponent. You don't want to double him up, of course, but sometimes you have to take that risk. You gotta have heart, as the old song goes.

If you have three times the big blind, just calling is never correct at this level—no matter what two cards you have. If you play a hand, you're going for all your chips. In no-limit hold'em, you cannot be afraid to go broke. You just say to yourself, "I'm short, I've gotta get more chips, so I've just gotta make a stand." If you get called, there's a chance that you have the worst hand, particularly when you've taken your stand with an inferior hand, so you just hope that you can draw out. When you raise all-in, you are simply making a calculated gamble that your opponents don't have a hand that they can call you with. You're trying to make the most of a bad situation.

Playing When You Are Short-Stacked

You gamble more with a short stack than you do with a big stack. Why? Because you're forced to do it. You have to change your chip position.

When you're the short stack there's only one direction to go—up. You're already at the bottom, you want to get to the top, and the only way to get chips is to fire. You're going to change your position one way or the other—you'll either go out the door or you'll get more chips. With a short stack you have to take more chances and become super aggressive.

Attacking the Big Stack

Now, suppose you are playing three-handed and the blinds are $100/$200. In this scenario, you have a little more flexibility. With $1,250 in chips, you can afford to take the blinds once before you have to make a move and still have $950 in chips, which is enough to play with.

You would rather attack the big stack's blind with a raise before the flop than the opponent with the chip count equal to yours. Your equal-chipped opponent is more likely to play with you since he already has $200 in the pot, whereas the one with the big stack is more likely to fold in the blind since he has plenty of chips to play with. In other words, the big stack is not committed to the pot, but the equal stack will be more likely to take a stand. Therefore you have a better shot at winning the pot uncontested against the tall stack than against the short stack. Just winning the blinds at this stage is critical because it can improve your chip position substantially.

Playing Premium Hands

Now, suppose you're lucky enough to be dealt a premium hand such as a big pair, A-K, A-Q, or even A-J. In this scenario you don't care who you go in against, although you might prefer going against the shorter stack—assuming that he calls your all-in raise—because if you win the pot, you will knock him out and have equal chips to the big stack. Heads-up, you will have at least a 50 percent chance of winning the satellite or even better odds if you think you are a better player than your opponent. Remember that when you start with 25 percent of the chips, you are only two pots away from winning the satellite.

Round Six

The blinds are $200/$400 with $5,000 chips in play (usually). If by accident, the satellite goes to the sixth level, the blinds will be so high that on virtually every hand all your chips will be in before the flop. There is no limping.

You know you're going to get called almost every time you raise, so you have to take at least a reasonable hand and go with it. You don't have much time to wait when you're heads-up, and it can get to the point where you and your opponent know that you're both pretty much going to go all-in on the next hand. And that is one of the reasons why you make a deal at this point or, if you would rather just flip a coin, you can go for it. Some players don't like to make deals, or they don't understand the concept of deal making. Of course one of the benefits of not making a deal is that you can never make a bad deal. Learning to negotiate a good deal is an important skill that must be learned.

Adjusting Your Strategy for Three-Handed Play

If you are three-handed when you get to the sixth level, where the blinds are $200/$400, your strategy will sometimes depend on how much money the tournament seat you are playing for is worth. The more the satellite is worth, the more willing you might be to make a settlement, assuming that the chips are fairly equally divided among the final three players.

If the chip counts are quite lopsided and you have a short stack, you don't have much strength to negotiate a deal, so you are likely to play the satellite to its conclusion. If you have a medium stack, you might try to negotiate some sort of save, perhaps for the amount of the buy-in at least. If you have the chip lead, you may opt to offer a reasonable settlement to your opponents to guarantee that you win the lion's share of the satellite money. Or if you have a huge chip lead, you might decide to just play it to the end without giving up anything.

"Whether you offer a deal when you are the chip leader might also depend on your financial condition," Tom adds. "If losing the satellite will mean that you can't play the tournament, you may be more likely to give up a piece of the action so that you can play the tournament. However if you're in good financial shape and are going to play the tournament no matter what happens in the satellite, you can base your decision on what you think is best economically speaking."

Let's look at a scenario in which you're going to play the satellite to its conclusion. With $5,000 in chips in play and the blinds at $200/$400, Player A has $2,500, Player B has $1,250, and you have $1,250. What is your strategy? We suggest that you go all-in before the flop on almost any hand that you decide to play. If you take both of the blinds, one-half of your chips will be gone, cutting your stack down to $650. If that happens, then you go in against an opponent and double up, you will only have about the same number of chips you had before the blinds. For that reason, you need to get your money in before you go through both blinds to give yourself a better chance of improving your chip position. You almost always will have to play something, except the most hopeless of hands. If you have a truly hopeless hand, trash such as 8-3, you will have to let it go, but with any semblance of a hand—any ace, any two cards 10 or higher, any pair, any suited connectors—you will be forced to play and take your chances.

"When it gets to $200/$400 and I am the first to act, I will move in with king-anything," Brad notes. "K-9 and K-8 are questionable, but still they're better than a random hand."

"If I am in an inferior chip position, I will take more risks," Tom adds. "I might move in with a 10-8 suited or a similar hand when I am the aggressor. I'm not talking about calling with these types of hands, I'm talking about the times when I can make a big enough raise to get my opponents to lay down their hands."

In other words, when you are first to act, you can play a lot worse hand than you can if you are a caller. You can put your opponent to the test, rather than the other way around.

Adjusting Your Strategy for Heads-Up Play

When you are heads-up with the blinds at $200/$400, the satellite becomes a blind-stealing event, strictly a move-in game. Even when you're still playing three-handed at these high blinds, one player steals, then the next player steals, and so on, until a player wakes up with a hand that he decides to play against an opponent that he thinks is trying to steal. In these types of situations, A-10 might look like a calling hand if you think that your opponent probably has a worse hand and is on a steal. You have to gamble more three-handed. You cannot allow yourself to get run over.

"If an opponent keeps putting me to the test relentlessly," Tom comments, "I'm going to have to take a stand sooner rather than later because if I let him pick up my big blinds twice, he'll be the one with the better chip position, and I'll be the guy hanging on by my fingernails. I can't allow that to happen, so with any reasonable hand I will take a stand."

Now, suppose you are heads-up in the big blind and your opponent limps in from the small blind. With any hand that is better than the average random hand—any ace, any king, any pair—you probably will move in. Typically, if you have a hand that is queen-high, you have a slightly above average random hand for heads-up play.

"I'm not going to move in with a hand like K-3 or Q-2," Tom says. "I will just wait and see the flop with those types of hands, unless I am convinced that the small blind will fold before the flop if I move all-in. I just have to make a correct judgment."

Usually when an opponent limps in from the small blind in heads-up play, he has one of two types of hands:

1. A strong hand that he's trying to trap you with; or
2. A marginal had that he wants to see the flop with.

Poker always requires making a judgment. Will my opponent call or won't he? If you firmly believe that he will fold, you can make a play at the pot, no matter what type of hand you have. You're gambling all your chips that he won't call. The only type of hand he will call you with is a strong hand. The chances are better that he has nothing, so you are the favorite to pick up the pot.

Playing Big Hands

Now, if you have a big hand — say, two aces or two kings — and he limps in from the small blind, you're more willing to give him a free flop. You hope that he makes a pair or something on the flop, a hand good enough that he will go in for all his chips. Of course, if you think that he will call a raise before the flop, go ahead and raise with your premium hand. Depending on the experience of your opponent (that is, how talented you think he is), you would rather make a mini-raise the size of the big blind to try to sucker him in. If he calls the mini-raise, he is more likely to be willing to commit after the flop because he already has a lot of chips in the pot. Sometimes he will even bet on the flop, no matter what comes, in an effort to pick up the pot. If you think that your opponent is very clever and will either fold or move in against a mini-raise, you will have to decide what type of hand he limped with. Is he trying to trap you? If you think he is trapping, you might just let him do it and then go after him on the flop.

What if you have pocket aces or kings in the small blind? Would you limp or raise? Ask yourself, "How can I get the most money into this pot?" One option is to make a mini-raise, double the amount of the big blind. Or if you're against a very aggressive player you might just limp with your big pocket pair. Why? Because you know that he probably will try to blow you out of the pot. By letting him raise, you will have him right where you want him. Then, consider raising the minimum amount—the size of the big blind—unless your opponent is super aggressive, in which case you can just call and give him the opportunity to hang himself.

"I'm a bit reluctant to let a random blind hand come in for free when I have a big pair," Tom comments, "because I never know where they're at and they can out-flop me. Also, the smaller my pocket pair, the more likely I am to just move in on the pot."

Again, use your best judgment when you have a big hand in the big or small blind heads-up. Use whatever strategy you believe will be most effective in getting the maximum amount of chips in the pot. You're going to the river, so you want to get all the chips in, knowing that you can't start with a better hand than pocket aces. If he draws out on you, that's just too bad.

"Even if I have two black aces and the flop comes with three hearts and he moves in on me," Tom says, "I'm forced to call him. I may not like it a whole lot, but I'm gonna have to put my money in and take my chances."

As a poker poet once wrote, "You push in your chips and pray/ That all of the others will throw away."

No-Limit Hold'em
Super Satellites:
Winning Strategies
Round-by-Round

8

This discussion is based on the structure of the super satellites held at Binion's Horseshoe during the World Series of Poker. The buy-in for the championship event at the World Series is $10,000, as is the buy-in for the championship event at other big tournaments such as Jack Binion's World Poker Open in Tunica and Bellagio's major tournaments. The super satellite format is almost the same for all tournaments that have a $10,000 buy-in. Super satellites for $10,000 events cost $200 to enter plus the vig. You begin with $200 in chips, and the rounds last twenty minutes. The format of satellites for $5,000 championship events is the same except that the buy-in and rebuys usually are $100 less.

Super satellites are similar to football games in that they have four quarters of play. The first quarter of a super satellite consists of the first three levels of play and is the rebuy period. At the end of this quarter, the super satellite truly begins. The second quarter is composed of levels four through seven, when you're trying to stay alive and accumulate some chips. The third quarter includes levels eight, nine, and ten (depending on the number of players in the event), when you are jockeying for position. The fourth quarter is the final table play.

Rebuys and Add-Ons

During the first three levels of play, you can rebuy any time you fall to $200 or less in chips. Rebuys cost $200, for which you receive an additional $200 in chips. At the end of the rebuy period, you can buy a single or double add-on, no matter how many chips you have in front of you. For example, if you have $200 or less in chips at the end of the rebuy period, you can take a $200 rebuy plus a double add-on. In that case, you will wind up with $800 in chips. When the rebuys and add-ons have been completed, all the $5 chips are raced off. After a 10-minute break, the fourth level begins with the blinds at $25/$50.

Factors to Consider Before You Rebuy

People use a variety of rebuy strategies in super satellites. When it comes to buy-in and rebuy strategies, there are five types of players:

1. One buy-in only players;
2. One buy-in plus one rebuy players;
3. One buy-in plus one or more add-ons players;
4. Unlimited rebuy players; and
5. Players who wait until the break to buy in to the satellite.

Some players make a onetime investment of $200 and try to win it with no rebuys. Some players are willing to rebuy once if they go broke early in the satellite. Others try to survive the rebuy period with one buy-in and then take the add-ons if they need to. A few players rebuy every time they get broke, sometimes on every hand they play. And some players even wait until the break to make their initial buy-in of $200, at which time they also pay $200 for a rebuy and $400 for a double add-on. In other words, they buy into the super satellite for $800.

Suppose you have budgeted $400 to invest in a super satellite. Tom believes that if you get broke early in the satellite, during the first round of play, for instance, when nobody has an overwhelming chip position yet, a rebuy definitely is in order. However, if someone has already racked up $1,200 in chips, which occasionally happens when a player goes on a big rush, you might think twice about rebuying. There are two schools of thought on this issue:

1. You have a much better chance of getting a hold of some chips if you're going up against a bigger stack.
2. You're going to be so far out-chipped that continuing to play isn't worth making a rebuy.

But as a general rule, no one accumulates a giant stack during the first round of play. Therefore you should ask yourself these questions when you get broke in the first level:

1. What kind of table am I at?
2. How tough are the players?
3. How much do they gamble?

Say that someone has won a lot of chips. Is he a good player? A bad player? Does he have position on you? If a bad player with a lot of chips is sitting to your right, you're much more inclined to rebuy. Or you might even add on if you think he's going to put his money in with weak hands. In that case, you can turn $400 into $800 with just one bet if you are able to get all your chips in.

On the other hand, if a real tough player with a big stack is sitting behind you, you might ask yourself, "Do I really want to gamble with rebuys when a tough player has position on me and a lot more chips that I have?" Sometimes it might be better to just wait for the next satellite. During the WSOP there usually are two super satellites a day, so you can decide to pass on rebuying and play the next super instead. The last three days, the Horseshoe offers three satellites a day, so you have plenty of opportunities to play one.

"I think it's foolish to get in for more than $600," Tom states, "although I've gotten in for as much as $800 a couple of times. I think that $200 to $600 is all that you should be willing to invest in one super satellite."

An investment of $200 to $400, plus the $25 vig, should give you a fairly good shot if you start the super satellite in round one. Don't forget, too, that you can play a one-table satellite for $1,000, plus the vig, and you only have to beat nine players. So you have to ask yourself, "Would I rather risk a lot of money in this super satellite, or would it be better to play a one-table satellite that costs $1,030?" This should be a factor in your thinking.

The First Quarter

The first quarter consists of three levels. In the first level of play, the blinds are $5/$10. In the second round, the blinds rise to $10/$20, and the third round blinds are $15/$30.

Round One

A lot of players play faster and gamble more in rebuy super satellites than they would in one-table freezeout satellites. It's not necessarily a bad thing for you if your opponents play this way, because when they're playing loose, it's easier for you to get the best of it. If you're playing a little bit conservatively, it isn't difficult to find a hand where you will have the advantage, and you should be able to get your money in when you have the edge. Therefore, a good strategy at the start is to play conservatively, look for a spot where you can get it all in and double up, and protect your chips if you are able to accumulate a big stack.

You usually will see more wild gambling in the first round than in the second and third rounds. Some players have the "no fear" mentality, and they'll take pocket fours, for example, and shove in all their chips. In fact a lot of players seem to have no problem putting all their chips in the middle with any two cards. If they get broke, they just reach in their pocket and pull out more money. They aren't concerned about making multiple rebuys and how much the super satellite might cost them. Of course we all know that even a loose or weak player can wake up with two aces. More likely than not, though, when a player goes to the center a lot more often than he should, he's gambling with marginal hands. Usually, players who are playing this way are simply trying to build up a good-sized stack, not really caring if it costs them a lot. If you choose this style of play and get a hold of chips early, we recommend that you change gears and move into the protection mode in order to keep them.

Designing a Workable Strategy for the First Round

Suppose you are planning to take only one rebuy. What type of strategy will work best for you? We suggest taking a conservative approach. During the first level of play, players do a lot of limping, so this is a time when you might speculate by putting in $10 to see some flops when you are in late position and can play a multiway pot. You won't be trying to steal $15 worth of blinds unless you have some kind of hand.

Try to get a quick line on other people's play. Because there often is a lot of loose-aggressive play in the first round, try to avoid putting in a lot of chips before the flop unless you have a premium hand. If you have a strong hand, especially if your opponents are gambling, be willing to push it. Although you might occasionally try to trap an opponent, you don't slow-play when your opponents are gambling. Put in a raise and hope that somebody who has a hand will come after you.

Just remember that a lot of players are willing to gamble, and they don't always need to have much of a hand to come after you. Some people have the "I want chips" mentality and don't care if they take the worst of it trying to get them. This is a good reason to take a conservative approach and play only premium hands during the first level. Try to at least hold even or tread water because you don't want to lose chips. Remember, the blinds are $5/$10 for twenty minutes, so you don't usually go through the blinds more than twice. If you don't play a single hand in the first round, you probably will still have at least $170 left to start the second round. Depending on where the high card sets the button and the speed of the game, you actually may have to post the blinds only once in the first round.

You're playing no-limit poker, and you can change your position very quickly. If you have $170 and double up one time, you'll have $340. Then, if you double up again, you'll have $680. You've gone from having just a few chips to having plenty. By waiting for hands, being patient and selective, you can improve your position.

You should also consider playing multiway pots, especially when you are in late position. You can play some speculative hands such as small pairs and suited connectors, but play them cheaply. You would prefer to see the flop before putting any serious money into the pot. If someone raises after you have limped with this type of hand, you usually should fold.

Also note that some players have been very successful playing the supers with a loose and aggressive strategy. They gamble and sometimes they get a hold of a lot of chips. They make up their minds that they're going to get chips, no matter how much it costs. If they put $800 to $1,000 into the super, is the risk worth the reward? If they win a seat, it is, although most of the time, they're going to crash and burn.

At the end of the rebuy stage, we believe that you need to have $800 or more to be comfortable. With $800 in chips, you have sixteen times the big blind–you're in good shape and there is no need to rebuy or add on. This is the main reason some players make their initial buy-in at the end of the rebuy period. They believe that they will avoid the risk of getting in deeper than $800 by rebuying and adding on whenever they get broke. They know that $800 is enough chips to play with when the blinds are $25/$50 at the start of round four.

Round Two

The blinds are $10/$20, which causes the chips to move around a little faster. Say that you sat out the entire first round, and which means you probably went through the blinds twice. You're sitting on $170 now. With the blinds at $10/$20, if you go through the blinds once, you're down to $140. If you go through them twice, you'll have

$110. In other words, you have to start looking for a hand to play.

You have to concentrate on the blinds and how they are affecting your stack. You can't let yourself get too short, so you're going to have to make a move. You have to hold there if you haven't found a hand. Often, you make a move when you can make a positional play with a medium-strength hand such as a K-J, which usually is a trouble hand. Say that you're sitting two spots in front of the button and no one has entered the pot. In that case you might take a shot with your K-J.

"That's my favorite hand," Brad says. "It's the hand that I won the World Series with. Of course I was playing heads-up, but I also broke the third-place finisher with a K-J."

Or you might play a hand that isn't that strong, such as 10-9 suited, and try to pick up the blinds against players that you think will fold. If they've been paying attention and notice that you haven't played a hand during the first and second levels, they will have to think twice before calling your raise. The point is that with the blinds going up, you have to make some sort of move to change your chip position. It's either double up or get broke, and then you've got to decide whether or not you want to rebuy and continue playing the satellite.

"My criteria for rebuying in the second level,"

Tom advises, "is somewhat similar to the first level. If the good players don't have a lot of chips, I'm more willing to take a rebuy. But if the better players have a ton of chips, I'm more willing to give it up."

Of course, other players might want to gamble and take a double rebuy when they get broke in the second level.

"Because the $30 in blinds per round is a fairly significant chunk of your chips (you only get $200 for a rebuy)," Brad adds, "I think it's very important to look at my position at the table, where I am sitting in relation to when I have to take the blinds again. If I get broke on the button, I'm going to rebuy because I'll get plenty of free hands to look at before I have to post the $20 big blind. But if I'm the next player to post the blinds, I just say 'See ya later,' and make plans to play the next satellite."

Our thinking is that when you go broke on the button, you'll get to look at seven or eight more hands if you rebuy. You'll have a chance to double up and get full value for your $200 in rebuy chips. Remember that you do not pay a vig on your rebuys.

Now suppose you have doubled your stack in the second level of play. Now you want to protect your chips and not gamble too much. You want to look for solid hands and good positional plays. You can go up against the players who are way out of line, and you'll have no problem finding them, either, during the first three levels of play. There is a wide range of ability levels in super satellites. You'll see world champions trying to win their way in on the cheap, and you'll see rank beginners gambling just for the thrill of playing.

"It's a great place for everybody to mix it up," Brad notes. "You get to play against all types of players."

Round Three: Your Last Chance To Rebuy

"The deeper I am into the third level, the less willing I am to gamble with a rebuy," Tom says, "because the $200 in chips is going to look relatively insignificant, considering how fast the blinds are going up."

The blinds are $15/$30, so you're going to lose $45 after taking the blinds once. If you've got $200 in chips, that's almost one-fourth of your stack. And by the third level, when a lot of players have doubled or tripled their chips, you're going to be way out-chipped. You might consider rebuying, however, if you're at a table where your opponents—even the big stacks—are doing a lot of gambling. In that case, you might decide that you have a chance to double or triple up if you rebuy. Again you must consider how soon you will have to take the blinds.

"It's like tiptoeing through land mines when

you're still in the rebuy stage," Brad says. "Everybody's firing at you. Unless you've played a few supers, it's hard to understand what a different ball game it is during the first three levels."

The playing field is no longer level at this point. You might be better off taking the $200 you'd have to pay for a rebuy, add the juice, and sign up for another satellite where you can start fresh on a level playing field. Remember that if you're ten minutes into the third round, it will only be ten more minutes before the blinds rise to $25/$50. And it's very difficult to accumulate enough chips to be competitive unless you're prepared to take one or more add-ons.

Say that you're in the satellite for the original $225. If you get broke during the third level, you will have to take a rebuy to stay in action. And then to be competitive, you'll probably need to take a double add-on. Now your investment has risen from $225 to $825. So are you better off saving your rebuy and add-on money at this late stage?

"Yes, unless it's the last super satellite before the Big One starts," Brad advises. "Then you say, 'Hey, I need all the fire power I can get. I've gotta gamble if I want to win a seat.' This one factor can change everything."

The last day or two before the Series begins, it's almost like a feeding frenzy. Where four to six seats had been given away in previous supers, suddenly there are as many as fifteen seats up for grabs. Now you have a lot more reason to gamble!

Setting your rebuy strategy in your mind before the super satellite begins is very important. Some people get WSOP fever and they just keep reaching for more money. It is much better to design a rebuy plan before you play the satellite. In some respects, playing a super satellite is similar to playing a low-limit rebuy tournament in that it's gamble-gamble. Sometimes it seems like nobody is willing to lay down a hand.

"I've seen players get into a time warp," Brad observes. "And every other hand, it seems like they're rebuying. Pretty soon they're in for a lot of money."

The Second Quarter
Round Four: You Have To Change Gears

No more rebuys. After a ten-minute break, all the $5 chips are taken out of play, and the blinds rise to $25/$50. The tournament changes—now people really begin to play in earnest. And an amazing thing often happens: Players begin breaking out at a rapid pace.

Usually the play will settle down after a few minutes, and players actually start playing poker. Now a raise means something, just like it does in a normal tournament, and players usually begin to slow down.

Of course, players who have gotten stuck in the mindset of sticking in their chips recklessly do not make the transition, and they continue to put in their money with marginal hands. They don't understand this basic principle of rebuy tournament play: You have to change gears after the rebuy period is over. They don't realize that you need to settle down and play solid poker because if you get broke, you can't rebuy and you will bomb out of the satellite. During the rebuy quarter, these aggressive or loose players participated in the feeding frenzy when everybody was firing in their chips on all sorts of hands. Because they don't change gears, many of them crash and burn early in the second quarter. But smart players settle down and nibble instead of gulp now that the feeding frenzy has died down.

You want to be very selective about the hands you play in round four. Say that you have $800 in chips. Although you would be in good shape with that many chips, the blinds are fairly high in relation to your $800. If you make one raise of $150 to $200, you will have around 25 percent of your chips in the pot. Now suppose an opponent comes over the top of you for $200 more. If you had enough of a hand to raise with, you're going to have to play for $200 more.

It is important to know how many chips your

opponents have in front of them. When you are heads-up, the biggest bet that you or your opponent can make is the amount of chips in the smallest stack, whether it is yours or your opponent's. For example, if you have $1,000 and your heads-up opponent has $2,000, he can't bet the $2,000, because you can only call $1,000 of the bet. So the limit in this situation is $1,000.

Try to figure out when your opponent is committed to the pot. It would not be wise to put in a raise with a marginal hand in an attempt to steal the pot when your opponent has a large percentage of his chips already in the pot. Before you raise in a situation like this, ask yourself, "Is he pot-committed?"

Again we remind you that you must continually perform the balancing act. Your table position, the quality of your hand, the nature of the players yet to act behind you, the amount of chips they have, how likely an opponent is to gamble with you— you must take all these things into consideration. If your opponents are in a gambling mode, you need to have a better hand because you know that you're going to get played with. You don't want to raise with a marginal hand like Q-10 when you're sure that an opponent is likely to play with you and probably has a better hand. Or suppose you raise with a marginal hand and someone comes over the top of you. The pot may be laying you 4 to 1, so you might be forced to call because you're getting the correct odds. You created the situation when you raised with a marginal hand, and now you're getting the right price to call the reraise—but you shouldn't have put yourself in that situation to begin with.

Our suggestion is that you adopt a conservative strategy, playing snugly, even treading water, trying to pick off players who are out of line when you have a good hand. You hope to gather a few chips if you can, but it isn't of the utmost importance. Staying alive is the important thing at this level. Remember that the field thins rapidly during the fourth level of play. A lot of players who used the no-rebuy strategy probably squeezed into the second quarter with $200 to $300 or even less, and the $25/$50 fourth level of play often makes a heavy hit on their chips.

Round Five

The blinds double to $50/$100—this is a big jump. During the fourth and fifth rounds, expect more than half of the field to bust out of the satellite. By the end of the fifth round, the survivors usually will have a decent amount of chips in front of them. Your normal raise during this round should be three to four times the size of the big blind, $300 to $400 in chips. Whenever you enter a pot, you should be prepared to commit the rest of your stack.

Or say that you have only $600 in chips. In that case, if you're going to play a hand, just move in with all your chips. Why? Because if you raise the normal amount, you will have over half your chips already in the pot, so you might as well go for your entire stack. In other words, if your hand is good enough to play with only $600 left in your stack, you should go for it.

Naturally, there is an exception. If you have precisely aces or kings, you may want to make only the standard raise because, with a hand that strong, you want to get some action. With pocket queens or jacks, we suggest that you raise all-in to deter an opponent who has a hand such as A-K, A-Q, or A-J from coming into the pot. Of course they probably will call you anyway, but that's okay too. In super satellites, a lot of situations are similar to flipping a coin. A pair against two overcards is very common. Sometimes you'll even be looking for a coin-toss hand yourself, if it is the best situation for you to play, because of your table position and your stack size. In other words, you may be in a spot where you have to improve your chip position and win some chips even if it means playing in a coin-toss situation.

Round Six

By the sixth round, expect about 50 percent or more of the field to be gone. Rather than doubling, the blinds usually rise to $75/$150, which slows things a bit so that you get a little more play for your chips. Playing a round costs $225, which means that the blinds are quite important. If you have $600 in chips, only four times the amount of the big blind, you are beginning to get in trouble and need to make a move to improve your chip position.

You might raise, trying to pick up a pot uncontested. Try to evaluate which players don't defend their blinds. They are the ones you want to attack. Even with a weaker hand, you might move in on someone that you don't think will call. If someone does call, you might get lucky and draw out if you have the worst hand. Sometimes it's either make a move or get anted out. Continually look for a hand or the best opportunity to pick up the pot uncontested.

Round Seven

At the beginning of the seventh level, the $25 chips are raced off. The blinds increase to $100/$200, a rather modest increase. As a general rule, approximately 25 percent of the field is still in action. You will be jockeying for position during this round, because the eighth level of play, when the blinds double to $200/$400, will make or break most of the remaining field. Realize that the next level is crunch time—if you have only $1,200 going in to level eight, you will have only three times the amount of the big blind, so you must amass some chips to get ready for the next round.

If you are successful during the seventh round, you will have a good chance of making it to the final table, or at least very close to it. It would be nice to have more than $2,000 in chips at the end of this level.

The Third Quarter
Round Eight

It's crunch time, and the blinds double to $200/$400, the biggest jump in the entire satellite. It's usually either double up or get up. Stealing the blinds becomes even more important because the blinds can eat up your stack. You have to open up your play and go for them. There are a lot of move-ins before the flop with no callers or only one caller, so you see very few flops. You seldom see a three-way pot. At this point in the satellite, most hands are raised. If you have $2,500 or less in chips and are the first one in the pot, you will probably move all-in—unless you have a big hand such as aces or kings, in which case you could limp in an effort to get some action.

When you are in the eighth round, you can count your chips to determine approximately where you are and where you need to be in order to win a seat in the $10,000 main tournament. For example, if you have $3,000 you have 30 percent of a seat. If you have $4,000, you have 40 percent of a seat. If you can build to about $6,000 or $7,000 in chips, you will be close enough to winning a seat that you will want to protect your chips. In other words, at each level you need to determine what your chip position is in relation to your opponents. Knowing where you are in relation to the table average will tell you whether you need to gamble and open up your play in order to get more chips, or whether you need to protect the chips you already have in order to make it to the final table. The shorter your stack, the more risk you need to take. The bigger your stack, the less risk you should take, playing mainly premium hands.

At the $200/$400 level, the satellite usually is down to two or three shorthanded tables, unless the field is massive. The normal field has ten to fifteen tables, 100 to 150 players, but a few days before the WSOP championship event begins, the fields often are twice as big.

Round Nine

The blinds rise to $300/$600, a 50 percent increase. If you have a very big stack at this point, you want to protect it. You don't want to play a big pot unless you have a premium hand. With a short stack, you just have to gamble if you want to improve your chip position. You don't have enough time to sit back and wait.

You will be playing according to the designated number of seats that are being awarded. Usually, a few spots also are awarded some cash.

"I played a super satellite for the 2003 Jack Binion World Poker Open that awarded four tournament seats," Tom says. "When we were six-handed, a player who was rather unknowledgeable about satellite strategy moved in before the flop. I threw away pocket queens without hesitation because I had enough chips to either win a seat or at least get very close. Within a few hands, we lost a player. As soon as we were five-handed, the same player who had raised all-in when I had the queens said, 'I don't want to play the tournament, so just give me the fifth-place prize money and you guys take the seats.' To my disbelief, one player actually considered not taking the deal! 'Please take this deal,' I begged. It was the best deal I'd ever heard of."

Suppose the satellite is down to six players and four seats are up for grabs, plus some cash for players who don't win a seat. In this situation you might lay down pocket aces before the flop. It sounds strange, but it sometimes is the correct play. For example, suppose you're playing six-handed and four seats are being given away. Fifth place pays $1,000, and sixth place says $800. You are the chip leader and have just been dealt pocket aces. An opponent who has only half as many chips as you moves in before the flop. Two other players at your table are so short-stacked, they hardly have enough chips to take the blinds. If you call the all-in raise, you might break your opponent and win all his chips. But why take the chance of losing half your chips? You will be taking no risk whatsoever if you simply wait and let the short stacks go through the blinds, knowing that there's a good chance they won't survive. Unless those stacks double up time and again, you already have a tournament seat locked up whereas if you play the hand, you're gambling to lose your seat.

"A few years ago, the Bicycle Club ran a super satellite for its $10,000 buy-in Diamond Jim Brady tournament," Tom adds. "Two seats were being given away. When it was three-handed, Mike Hart and one of his opponents each had a mountain of chips and the third player had a tiny molehill. Hart moved in holding an A-K, and his big-stacked opponent called him with pocket queens. Hart almost fell out of his chair when he got called—he knew that the caller didn't have to do a thing to ensure winning a seat because the molehill was going to get blinded out in just a few hands. Fortunately, Hart spiked an ace and won the pot. But the point is that his opponent should have folded the pocket queens without hesitation."

It is difficult in satellites, as it is in live action, to figure out the logic of unknowledgeable players or weak players. Brad relates a similar satellite incident: "I had pocket aces in a super satellite for a seat in the $5,000 buy-in Four Queens Classic a few years ago in which four seats were being awarded. I was second in the chip count. The chip leader, who had no clue as to what he was doing, came after me with an all-in raise. I had pocket kings and I called him. He busted me with his A-K, leaving me with nothing. He had a huge amount of chips, and I was a distant second. He didn't seem to realize that he was jeopardizing his chances of winning a seat when he already had one locked up. Nobody at the table could have hurt me except him. It was a painful lesson to learn. People who make erratic plays are the types who sometimes break me."

Now suppose the satellite is down to nine players, five seats are being awarded, and the chips are fairly evenly distributed. In this case you still have to go through four players to win a seat, so you would play pocket aces.

The Fourth Quarter
Final Table Strategy: An Overview

In the typical 150-player satellite, the $400/$800 ninth level usually is the last round. Sometimes the satellite will go up to $600/$1200/ and eventually to $800/$1,600, but satellites that go that long usually have 200-plus players in the starting field, so there are more chips in play with higher blinds at the end.

Let's say that you're playing seven-handed and you're very close to the money. Everyone will change their play at this point. Survival mode kicks in. Now its very important to know who you can steal from and who you can't. Look for players who are just sitting there, posting the blinds, and waiting for somebody else to get broke.

Sometimes it's easier to steal from someone who has a lot of chips. Why? Because he is protecting them and is likely to throw away more premium hands, preferring not to go up against some of the goofballs who play bad and sometimes win with trash. For this reason, if you're short-stacked, you actually can go after the bigger stacks. As we've emphasized previously, short stacks must take more risks, putting their chips in jeopardy to try to improve their chip position. You simply cannot allow yourself to get blinded out of action.

At this point in the satellite, it's pretty much a move-in game. The short stacks usually move all their chips in when they play a hand. Everybody seems to take turns stealing the blinds until someone wakes up with a hand and calls an all-in raise. And that's usually the way that short-stacked players go out—they've been blinded down so low that they take a chance and then run into a better hand. You will see some short stacks making a lot of bad calls with inferior hands such as Q-J. If a short stack has an ace, he almost always pushes in his chips. It's almost like ace-and-race for the short stacks. They have to make a move because they cannot afford to take the blinds.

Although when you're short-stacked, you usually don't care if you have to go up against a big stack, but it depends on what type of player the big stack is. If he is more apt to call you, you might want to think twice before you go all-in. But if the big stack is in a protective mode, he usually will fold when a short stack raises all-in. Also, if a big stack has so many chips that he has a seat locked up no matter what, he will be more likely to try to take you off if you have a short stack.

Look around the table and ask yourself, "Who do I want to attack? Who at this table will lay down the biggest hand if I move in?" That's the player you want to take a chance against. You might even go after him with nothing; if he has a hand, it's just too bad for you. When you're short-stacked, you either have to double up through somebody, or pick up enough blinds uncontested in order to stay alive. Actually if you can just win the blinds, you may get a shot at winning a seat. Things usually come to the point where you will be out of the satellite if you don't move in with your next hand.

In the following chapter, we give you specific

pointers and strategic tips on how to play the final table of a super satellite.

No-Limit Super Satellites: Playing the Final Table

by Brad Daugherty

9

You've made it to the final table and your concentration is in high gear. Now you need to decide what you want to accomplish and how you plan to do it. Will you be happy just making the money, or do you want to do everything you can to win a seat? Going full out to win the seat can get you broke early, but will give you a better chance of winning. I like going for the seat!

In order to improve your ability to read your opponents, ask yourself the following questions, the answers to which might be the keys to making correct decisions:

1. What are my opponents thinking at this point? Try to figure out the mindset of each of your opponents.
2. Which player is most likely to raise? It's usually the big stack who does the initial raising.
3. Who is afraid of losing and, therefore, is most likely to fold? Some players just wait for their opponents to bust out so that they can move up a notch

toward the money. These are the players you want to attack.

4. Who will fold a good hand? Players who are in the waiting mode sometimes will fold against an aggressive raise.

5. Who won't? The short stacks usually will play any decent hand because they need chips.

6. Depending on his position, how strong a hand would each of your opponents need to raise with? It's important to analyze table position and chip count. When a player raises, ask yourself why. Is he an aggressive player who is just trying to bully the game? If he's been playing tight, he is more apt to have a strong hand.

7. How strong a hand would each of your opponents need in order to call a raise? Many factors can affect a player's decision to call, including his chip count and the chip counts of his opponents. Identify who is trying to wiggle into the money, who is short and desperate, who is loose-aggressive, who is solid-aggressive, and who is a calling station.

8. If someone limps, what kind of hand do you think he might have? You don't see much limping at the final

table, so when someone limps from up front, red warning lights should flash in your mind. The limper could be sandbagging a big hand in an effort to check-raise someone in a later position.

9. If someone just calls a raise, ask yourself why. Does he want other players to also come into the pot? How many chips does he have? If the raiser has a small amount left, it is more likely that the smooth-caller has a big hand and wants you to come into the pot with him. If the raiser has a big stack and the smooth-caller also has a big stack, it is more likely that the caller would have reraised if he had a big hand so he could play heads-up against the raiser and possibly break him.

Marching Forward to the Battlefield

Now let's get on with playing the final table. During this discussion, I often will refer to myself as "we," which refers to you and me. I am your coach, and we are playing this satellite as one entity. We are Player 1 sitting in seat one with

$3,800. Study the diagram below to understand the big picture of the battlefield upon which we will lead our soldiers to war against our eight enemies.

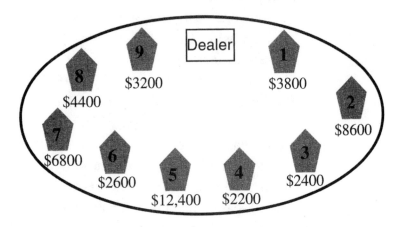

$10,000 Super Satellite Final Table
No-Limit Hold'em

100-Player Field	$20,000
78 Rebuys	$15,600
54 Add-Ons	$10,800
Total	**$46,400**

The Pay Schedule

1st	$10,000 seat + $300 cash
2nd	$10,000 seat + $300 cash
3rd	$10,000 seat + $300 cash
4th	$10,000 seat + $300 cash
5th	$2,500 Tournament Chips
6th	$1,250 Two Chips plus $250 cash
7th	$800 One Chip plus $300 cash
8th	$650 One chip plus $150 cash
9th	No payout

When we make the final table, we are still playing $400/$800 blinds. To start the action, the dealer high cards for the button to start. Player 4 draws the button, Player 5 puts in $400 for the small blind, and Player 6 puts in $800 for the big blind.

Player 4 is the shortest stack at the table, so drawing the button when the blinds are so high is a huge advantage for him. He will have a full round before he needs to make a serious decision, and he may easily get a premium hand to play in that time. It is also possible that one or more players may go broke before Player 4 has to make a decision, thus allowing him to at least make the money, as only eight players get paid. Winning $650 is much better than getting zero for ninth.

Player 6 now has only $1800 left after putting in the big blind. He must be considering what types of hands he might throw away and the kinds of hands he might call with. He has the small blind next and will have only $1,400 after posting it.

Hand One

The first hand is dealt and Players 7 and 8 pass. Player 9 moves in. We look at our cards:

We ask ourselves:

1. What would Player 9 have moved in with?
2. Could A-10 be the best hand?
3. Is Player 6 committed to the pot?

There are still five players to act behind us, including Player 6 with a short stack—$800 of his $2,600 is in the pot for the big blind. We decide to fold.

Everyone else folds around to the big blind, who does a lot of thinking. Finally he throws his hand away, leaving him with $1,800. Player 9 wins the pot uncontested and adds $1,200 to his stack, which now is $4,400.

Hand Two

Player 5 has the button, Player 6 posts the $400 small blind, and Player 7 puts in $800 for the large blind. Player 6 now has only $1,400 left in his stack.

"Who wants to make the money?" we wonder. Now that Player 6 is very short on chips, some players will throw their premium hands away to at least win the minimum of $650 for eighth place.

Players 8 and 9 muck their cards, and when it comes to us, we look down and find the:

We pause, thinking that if we put in a normal raise, we'll be committed anyway, and we don't want anyone to come over the top of us, thinking that we might lay it down. For that reason, we just move in. Our thinking is that we have enough chips that even the larger stacks don't want us to double through them and possibly switch positions with them. The short stacks will fold unless they have a very premium hand because they are looking to make the money. As long as no one has a big hand, we should win the blinds.

Everyone folds around quickly until it gets to the large blind. He studies for a while, flashes the K♥ Q♦, and folds. We add the $1,200 to our stack, giving us $5,000. Player 7 now has $6,000, and Player 6 is very short with only $1,400.

Hand Three

Player 6 has the button, Player 7 posts the $400 small blind, and Player 8 puts in $800 for the large blind. Everyone folds around to Player 5, the chip leader, who makes a standard raise of $2,400, three times the big blind. Everyone folds without hesitation, and Player 5 takes the pot uncontested. The chip counts are now as follows:

After just three hands, the two chip leaders, Players 5 and 2, have held their own. Player 7 has slipped as the result of taking just two blinds, but he is still in third place. We have moved up to fourth. Player 9 is now in fifth place as the result of winning the blinds just one time. Player 8 has slipped into sixth place after posting only the big blind. Players 3 and 4 remain in seventh and eighth place. Player 6 has lost the most and is now in ninth place simply because he was unlucky enough to be the first player to have to post the two blinds.

Hand Four

The fourth hand begins with Player 7 on the button. Player 8 posts the $400 small blind, and Player 9 posts the $800 big blind. Everybody now passes to Player 5, our chip leader, who again raises to $2,400. Everybody folds, demonstrating once again that chips are power.

Hand Five

As the fifth hand begins, Player 8 has the button, we are in the $800 big blind, and Player 9 is in the $400 small blind. The action passes all the way around to Player 9, who decides to call the additional $400. We are holding the:

We decide to try to pick up the pot right here. Player 9 has only $2,800 left in his stack, so we move in for the rest of his chips. Player 9 has a tough decision to make. If he had a strong starting hand himself, he probably would have raised to start with. We are now putting him to the maximum test. If he calls and loses, he will go broke and get nothing. If we lose, we would still have enough chips left to remain in the hunt, although we would be short-stacked. This looks like a very good opportunity to pick up the pot. Player 9 mucks his hand. We now have $5,800 in chips.

Hand Six

Player 9 is on the button, we put in the ($400 small blind, and Player 2 posts the $800 large blind, making this his first time in a pot. Everyone folds around to Player 7, who also has yet to play a pot. He brings it in for $2,500. Being fourth in the chip count, Player 7 has the most to lose, so we have to give him credit for a real hand. Everyone folds to us in the small blind. We have A♠ J♣. Electing not to gamble, we fold. If we had been heads-up with the same hand against the big blind, we would have raised it, but it takes a stronger hand in order to call than it does to raise. Player 2 folds as well, and Player 7 wins the pot.

Hand Seven

We have the button, Player 2 posts the $400 small blind, and Player 3 posts the $800 large blind. Again Player 5 brings it in for a raise, making it $2,400 to go, an amount that would put Player 3, the big blind, all-in if he calls. Everyone folds to Player 3, and he thinks for a moment. Showing Q♥ J♦, he quietly tosses his hand in the muck. We figure that he probably would have played if one of the other players already had gone out, assuring him of a money spot.

It appears that Player 5 is putting maximum pressure on the pots because nobody wants to risk going broke against him. This is a very good strategy—until someone gets fed up and puts a stop to it by moving all-in against Player 5 and putting him to the test.

Hand Eight

Player 2 is on the button, Player 3 is in the $400 small blind, and Player 4 is in the $800 big blind as the eighth hand begins. Player 3 has only $1,200 left in his stack after posting the small blind, and Player 4 has $1,400 left after posting the big blind. This time we are hoping that everyone folds to us. We believe that Players 3 and 4 will throw away anything except a premium hand. Why? Because Player 6 has only $1,400 left, and he will more than likely go broke before either Player 3 or Player 4 have to play again.

Even before we look at our cards, we know that we are going to raise this pot if no one comes into it in front of us. The only thing that we have to fear is getting called or raised by Player 2. Everyone throws away to us. We look down to find J♥ 9♣ and raise it to $2,400. Player 2 thinks for a while, and then, to our pleasure, throws his hand away. Players 3 and 4 immediately fold their hands, and we add another $1,200 to our stack, giving us $6,600.

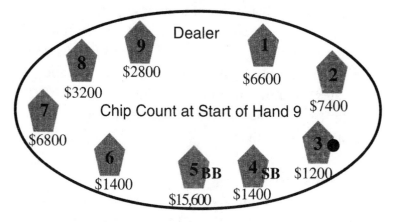

After Hand 8, Player 5 is still the leader. Note that Player 6 has $1,400, the same amount of chips as Player 4, but Player 6 is in a more perilous position because he has to post both of the blinds before the other short stacks do.

Hand Nine

Player 3 is the button. Player 4 posts the $400 small blind, leaving him with $1,000. Player 5, the leader, posts the $800 big blind, leaving him with $14,800. Everyone throws away until it gets to Player 2. He thinks about it a moment and makes a raise to $3,200. Players 3 and 4 throw away quickly. Player 5 hesitates for a while and says out loud, "You must have a big hand to raise me!" He then flashes the A♦ J♠ and throws them in the muck. Player 2 shows K♥ K♣ and rakes in the blinds.

Analyzing the situation, we realize that Player 2 had to have a big hand. Why? Because when he raised to $3,200, almost half of his stack, he was committed to the pot. With the three very short stacks at the table, he almost had to have a big hand to raise Player 5's big blind. Player 5, therefore, was correct in laying down the A-J. Perhaps he realized that with his superior chip position he had no need to gamble.

Hand Ten

At the start of the tenth hand the chip standings are: Player 5, $14,800; Player 2, $8,600; Player 7, $6,800; Player 1 (you and me), $6,600; Player 8, $3,200; Player 9, $2,800; Player 6, $1,400; Player 3, $1,200; and Player 4, $1,000. With three players having less than $1,400 each, somebody has to go broke soon.

On the tenth hand, Player 4 has the button, Player 5 has the $400 small blind, and Player 6 has the $800 big blind, leaving him with only

$600. It looks like he will have to play any two cards. Everyone would like to see him go broke so they can at least make the money. Everybody folds around to Player 5, thinking that he will raise. He doesn't disappoint them; he raises enough to put Player 6 all-in. Player 6 calls time and thinks and thinks. He then shows the 8♠ 3♥ and throws away. Players 3 and 4 both groan, wanting to see him go broke. We make a mental note, knowing that when Player 6 folded, his chances of winning a seat became slim to none.

Hand Eleven

Player 5 is on the button. Player 6 posts the $400 small blind, which leaves him with only $200. Player 7 posts the big blind of $800. Everyone throws away to me. We look around the table and realize that Player 6 probably is going to throw any hand away. Why? Because he knows that Players 3 and 4 cannot make it through the blinds without playing a hand. The short stacks are fighting to make the money.

We look down and find the:

I make the standard raise to $2,400. Everyone folds, including Player 6, who has only $200 left. Players 3 and 4 now know they're in trouble — they must take the blinds before Player 6 does.

The chip standings at the end of Hand 11 are: Player 5 is still in first with $15,600; Player 2 has $8,600; we are now in third place with $7,800; Player 7 is fourth with $6,000; Player 8 is fifth with $3,200; Player 9 is in sixth place with $2,800; Player 3 is seventh with $1,200; Player 4 is eighth with $1,000; and Player 6 is bringing up the rear with $200 in chips.

Hand Twelve

On the twelfth hand, Player 6 has the button, Player 7 posts the $400 small blind, and Player 8 posts the $800 big blind. Player 9 looks at his hand and moves all-in for $2,800. Everyone folds. A dozen hands have come and gone, and we still haven't seen a flop.

Hand Thirteen

Player 7 is on the button, Player 8 posts the $400 small blind, and Player 9 puts in $800 for the big blind. The time clock rings and the floorperson informs us that the blinds are going up to $600/$1,200 on the next hand. We look down to find garbage and muck the hand. Everyone throws away to Player 5, who raises to $2,400. Player 7 quickly pushes all his chips into the middle. The two blinds throw away their hands. Player 5 thinks for a while and then folds.

Hand Fourteen

We look around the table and analyze the situation. Here's how we see it: Player 5 is in the strongest position with $13,200. His best strategy is to just stay even—if he does, he will surely win a seat. Player 7 is also in very good shape with $9,200. Player 2 is in third with $8,600, and he also must be feeling confident. We are sitting in fourth chip position with $7,800, $1,200 of which is in the big blind. We're not in great shape, but we only need to win maybe one or two pots to win a tournament seat. Player 9 is in fifth place with $3,200, so he probably needs to more than double up to have a chance at a seat. Player 8 is in sixth with $2,000, and he definitely needs to double up, maybe twice, to have a chance at winning a seat. Player 3 is in seventh position with $1,200. He's in major trouble because his blind is coming up soon. Player 4 is in eighth place with $1,000, and he also has to post a blind shortly. With only $200, Player 6 is in last place and is just hoping the other short stacks get broke before he does. With virtually no chance of winning a seat at this time, he's just hoping to somehow jump up in the money.

At this point everyone would at least like to make the money. The way they play from here on out will show just how badly they want to win a seat, or whether they would be content with just taking home some money. Remember that our main goal is to win a seat, but we don't want to be too foolish and lose out on making as much as we can. The final four players get a seat no matter how many chips they have. The chip leader gets the same prize as the player who finishes fourth. No matter what the difference in chips, when the fifth player goes out the satellite is over.

When one player has a huge lead, you might not need to have as many chips as you ordinarily would need to win a seat. Since fewer chips are distributed among the rest of the players, the winners don't need to have as many chips as they might need if the chips were distributed more evenly. In our example, with four seats being awarded, the approximate number of chips needed to win a seat would be around $10,000.

As hand fourteen begins, Player 8 has the button. Player 9 is in the small blind and posts $600, and we have the $1,200 big blind. Everyone throws away around to Player 7, who raises to $3,600. Players 8 and 9 fold, so it's our turn to act. We look down and see the:

We would play this hand if we could be the raiser. It actually might be the best hand, but we don't really want to get broke in this spot. We believe that we would be better off waiting for another hand, so we throw the K-Q away. Notice that we have now played fourteen hands at the final table of this super satellite, and we still haven't seen any flops, which is a very common occurrence. But hey, it looks like we're going to see some flops real soon.

Hand Fifteen

On the fifteenth hand, Player 9 has the button, we post the $600 small blind, and Player 2 posts the $1,200 big blind. Player 3 is in very bad shape, so bad that he must play either this hand or the next one. If he has a K-9 or better, he is supposed to move in now, but if he doesn't have at least that good a hand, he should just wait and play the next hand when he'll be in the big blind. Of course, if he doesn't play, he's hoping that someone goes broke on this hand so he can at least make the money.

In fact, all of the short stacks are just trying to squirm into the money at this point. Players 8 and 9, the medium stacks, are going to wait for the shorter stacks to get broke, unless they pick up a big hand. Therefore, we'll be wary if they come into the pot. All the chip leaders just want to slowly grind away and not play any big pots unless they have a big hand. Everyone throws away to Player 7, who raises once again to $3,600. Everybody folds, and he picks up the blinds again. He seems to be getting more aggressive now that he has accumulated chips.

Hand Sixteen

On the sixteenth hand, we have the button, Player 2 has the $600 small blind, and Player 3 is forced to go all-in by posting the $1,200 big blind.

Player 4 moves all-in for $1,000, and Players 5 and 6 throw their cards in the muck. Player 7 now raises to $2,400. Everyone else folds to us. Now it's our turn to act, and we look down to find the A♠ K♠.

Wow, what a decision! Let's see, the big blind

is all in for $1,200, and Player 4, the other short stack, has gone all in for $1,000, so he must have a pretty good hand. Player 7, the one who has been doing a lot of raising, must have some kind of a hand. But it looks more like he is trying to isolate the two short players to himself. We have three choices:

1. Throw our hand away;
2. Just call the raise; or
3. Reraise.

What will give us the best chance to win this pot? We don't really want to put in $2,400 of our remaining $6,000 and then run away from it if we don't hit the flop. Player 7 has been doing a lot of raising lately, and we think we need to win at least one more pot in order to win a seat, which is our main goal. So we decide to move in, hoping that we have the best hand in case Player 7 calls us. We would prefer that he throw his hand away, thus allowing us to win the side pot, which is the separate pot created for the active players who still have chips to bet each other but is not shared by the all-in player, who has no more chips available. This also gives us a free roll for the main pot against the two short stacks.

We move in. Player 2 in the small blind folds. Player 7 thinks about it briefly, and then throws his hand away. Since both Player 3 and Player 4 are all-in, the three of us turn up our hands to see the first flop of the night.

Player 3

Player 4

Player 1

The Flop

The Turn   **The River**

4♦ ♦   5♠ ♠

♦ ♦♦   ♠

            ♥ ♥♥

But wait! After we made this play, we realize that we've overlooked something. Did you see it? It should have been obvious to us that one player had to have a premium hand—Player 4. Why? He put himself all-in in front of the big blind, who was already all-in. The signal was there, we just didn't read it. Player 4 had to have a strong hand to put his money in at this point. This is one of those times when making a mistake in judgment paid off—in other words, we got lucky.

Player 3 suffered the biggest heartbreak on this hand. He got very lucky by making trip fours on the turn with his trash blind hand, only to have his hopes crushed by the cruel 5♠ on the river that gave us the flush. Two people got broke on the hand. And because they both got broke going into the money, they split the eighth-place prize for $325 each.

Look at Player 6: he has a big grin on his face. With only $200 left in his stack, he has jumped into at least seventh place. He has made the most of his chips. We now take a count of everyone's chip position. Here's how things look going into hand seventeen:

Player 5 is still the leader with $13,200, and we are now in second chip position with $11,200. A smiling Player 6 sits in last place with $200 in chips, very happy to slide into the money. With over $10,000 in chips, we believe that all we need to do is just protect them, so we will try not to play many pots and let the short stacks bust out. Hopefully we can maintain our chips right around this amount, mainly just by picking up a few blinds to hold even.

Hand Seventeen

Since Player 3 and Player 4 went broke on the same hand and Player 2 has the button, there will only be one big blind—Player 5, who must post $1,200—with no small blind. Player 6 says, "Time to go!" and moves in his large stack of $200 with no worries, knowing that he has done everything that he was hoping for.

Player 7 folds, Player 8 folds, and then Player 9 moves all-in for $2,600. Everyone throws away around to Player 5 in the big blind. He finds a hand and calls. The players turn up their cards:

Player 5

Player 6

Player 9

The Flop

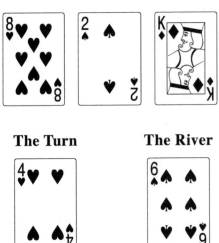

The Turn   The River

Player 6 finished in seventh place for $800. Player 9's pair of queens won him a nice pot and knocked Player 5 into second place with $10,600 in chips. It's now down to six players—just two more out and we win a seat.

Hand Eighteen

Since Player 5 had the large blind on the last hand, there will be a dead button—that is, the button stays where it was, and Player 2 gets the button for a second time. Player 5 will have to post the $600 small blind, and Player 7 must post the big blind of $1,200.

As the action begins, Player 8 moves all-in for $2,000. Player 9 immediately moves all-in behind him. The rest of us fold, including the blinds. Players 8 and 9 turn up their hands for the showdown.

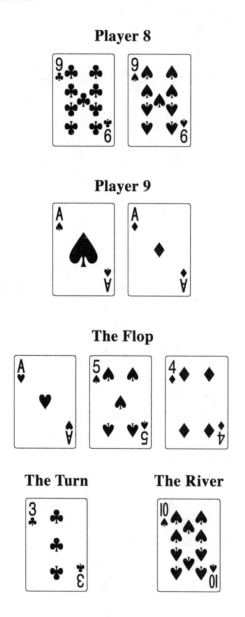

Player 8

Player 9

The Flop

The Turn

The River

Bad break for Player 8; he was drawing dead after the flop unless he could've caught two running nines for a win or a deuce and a trey for a split pot. He finishes in sixth place and receives $1,250.

We are now down to crunch time! The next player out gets $2,500 and everyone else gets a $10,000 seat in the Big One, plus $300 cash. The house usually awards some cash along with the seats, so that players will have money to tip the dealers and floor people.

Now all we need is for one more player to go broke, and we will win a seat—as long as it isn't us, that is. Now that we're down to five players, the chips have evened out a lot. We are now the leader with $11,200. Player 5 has $10,000. Players 7 and 9 both have $9,200, and Player 2 has $6,800.

Hand Nineteen

As the nineteenth hand is dealt, Player 5 has the button, Player 7 posts the $600 small blind, and Player 9 puts in $1,200 for the big blind. We look down and find the:

K-J is not a bad hand, but since we have plenty of chips, we would rather wait and see if someone gets busted. We fold. When Player 2 moves in, everyone else folds. The five of us are still very close in the chip count.

At this point, players sometimes will make a deal. For instance, the total prize pool for the final five places is $43,700. Divided by 5, that's $8,740 each. A fair deal would be something like this: All the players getting a seat would give fifth place $1,000. That way, the fifth-place finisher would lock up $6,500 instead of the $2,500 listed on the official payout sheet. The four players getting a seat would actually receive a $9,300 value. But today, one player doesn't want to make a deal, so we are going to play it out. Hang on!

Hand Twenty

Player 7 is the button. Player 9 has to post the $600 small blind, and we have to put in $1,200 for the big blind. Player 2 opens for a raise of $3,200. Everyone throws away. We look down to find the 7♠ 2♥. Ugh. We fold.

Hand Twenty-One

As this hand begins, Player 9 is the button, we have the $600 small blind, and Player 2 has the $1,200 big blind.

Player 5 moves all his chips in under the gun for $10,000. Player 7 calls all-in for $8,600. Player

9 throws away. Now it's our turn to act from the small blind. We look down at our cards and can't believe what we see—the A♠ A♥! Wow, this is weird—how can we lose with pocket aces?

But wait! Let's analyze this before sticking our chips in the pot. Player 5 must have a good hand to move in under the gun. And Player 7 must have a very good hand to call. Player 5 is all-in, and if he wins the pot, we get a seat. If Player 7 wins it, Player 5 will only have $1,400 left in his stack. If we call, we are giving ourselves a chance to come in fifth place, one away from winning a seat. Our best play is to muck these two aces. In the best scenario, Player 7 goes broke. If they have the same hand, we'll still have chips to play with. Why take a chance on coming in fifth? We fold. They turn their hands up.

Player 5

Player 7

The Flop

The Turn   ## The River

Both players make a straight and split the pot. If we had played our aces, we would have gone broke! Yes, folks, in this very special situation, it is correct to throw away A-A.

Hand Twenty-Two

On the next hand, we have the button, Player 2 has the $600 small blind, and Player 5 has the $1,200 big blind. Player 7 limps in for $1,200. Player 9 folds, and so do we. Player 2 calls in the small blind, and to our surprise, Player 5 raises $4,000 from the big blind, making it $5,200 to go. Answering the challenge, Player 7 moves all-in by raising it $4,300 more. Player 2 folds. Player 5 says, "I guess I have to go," and calls the raise. "What could Player 7 have?" we ask ourselves.

Our intuition about his suspicious limp proves correct when he shows:

Player 7

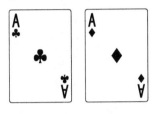

Player 5

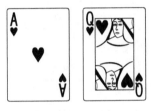

The Flop

The Turn

The River

Player 5, our chip leader throughout most of the super satellite, now has only $1,400 left after losing this pot.

As we think this hand through, we note that Player 5 had a legitimate hand here, but he should have heard a warning bell ring when Player 7 limped in—especially since everyone had been raising whenever they came into the pot before this hand came up. When Player 5 raised, he should have raised only three times the big blind. That way he could have laid down his hand when Player 7 came over the top for all his chips. Player 5 still would have had enough chips left to make a good raise on the next hand.

For many years I've been hearing players say, "I have to go." But you never really have to go, I guess, unless someone puts a gun to your head.

Hand Twenty-Three

When the twenty-third hand is dealt, Player 2 has the button. Player 5 posts the $600 small blind, leaving only $800 in his stack. Player 7 puts in $1,200 for the big blind. Player 9 folds, and we look down and are delighted to find a big hand:

We want to raise it, but we only want to play against Player 5. If we can break him, we'll win a seat. So we just double it to $2,400. We don't want to jeopardize any more than that in case someone sitting behind us wakes up with A-A. Player 2 folds.

Like a broken record, Player 5 says, "I gotta go!" and shoves in the rest of his chips. Player 7, who now has a huge lead, calls the other $1,200 from the big blind.

The flop comes:

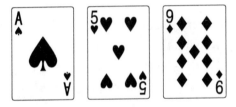

Player 7 checks the flop, then we check. The turn card is the:

We both check. The river card is the:

We both check. "Turn 'em up!" the dealer commands.

Player 5 shows the 9♣ 5♦ for two pair. Player 7 smiles and turns up the 9♥ 7♠ for a larger two pair.

In this final scenario, Player 7 understood as well as we did the wisdom of checking the hand to the end, thus allowing two hands to go against the all-in player. This strategy gave us a better chance to beat him. Which one of us broke him wasn't important, because we both would win a seat no matter who busted him. Player 5 left the table $2,500 richer.

Oh, I forgot to mention that upon Player 5's untimely demise, the satellite ended. And as a member of "The Final Four," we won a seat in the Big One. Yeah!

Online Satellites:
How to Play for
Profit and Pleasure

10

The games are the same, but online satellite play is different from on-land satellite play. One major difference is the number of chips that you start with in online satellites. Rather than the normal $300 to $500 in chips you get in on-land satellites, you usually start with between $1,000 and $1,500 in chips. In some respects, you get more bang for your buck in the online satellites that start you off with $1,500 in chips and fifteen-minute rounds in that you get to see almost twice as many hands, so you get a little more play for your buy-in. With more chips in play and more hands to look at, skill gains importance. Be sure to check your site's format, however, as some sites give you $800 in chips to start with and the limits rise after every ten hands.

Online vs. On-Land Tells

The 2003 World Series of Poker champion, Chris Moneymaker, won a $39 online satellite at PokerStars.com, parlaying it to $2.5 million at the

WSOP. Moneymaker mentioned in an interview that he had been able to figure out certain online tells that helped him win the satellite. This surprised some readers who assumed that since you can't see your opponents, online poker is void of tells. Wrong.

As an example, one online tell to watch for is the speed with which your opponents check their hands. Sometimes four or five players will check almost instantaneously when it's their turn to act. This means that they have clicked the check button and even the check-fold button in advance. This usually is a sign of weakness, which you can capitalize on in a future round of betting, especially in no-limit hold'em satellites.

Suppose the flop comes and you make a little pause before you click the check button. Three opponents go blip-blip-blip in rapid succession as they check around the table. You automatically know there is a good chance that they don't have anything, so when the next card comes, you have the opportunity to bluff at it if you want to.

Making a Deal

Another difference between on-land casinos and online casinos is the practice of deal-making at the end of satellites. In about 75 to 80 percent of on-land satellites, the final players make a deal at the end that redistributes the prize money. In online casinos there usually is no provision for chopping or making a save at the end of a satellite, which means that players have more incentive to go for the whole enchilada, so to speak. Some online casinos have a provision that allows players to make a deal at the end of a tournament, but people usually must play a satellite to its conclusion with no deal making.

Payouts

Online casinos usually take as many entries as they can get for satellites, similar to super satellites. The casino then awards as many tournament seats as possible, depending on the number of entries, and when there is any excess cash left over, they award it to the one final player who doesn't win a seat. Sometimes online casinos will award as many as twenty tournament seats from one satellite, with the twenty-first player receiving the odd money. These multi-table online satellites seldom have rebuys, while on-land super satellites always offer the opportunity to rebuy.

In 2003 PokerStars.com offered several online satellites for a $10,000 entry into the championship event at the World Series of Poker. In many cases, the site also added $2,000 cash to cover the winner's expenses at the WSOP, making the total package worth about $12,000. In on-land casinos, the most extra cash awarded to anyone who wins a seat in a super satellite usually is around $300.

Some online casinos pay three spots in one-table satellites. First place might win 50 percent of the prize pool, with second place winning 30 percent, and third place receiving 20 percent. One online site features $109 buy-in, one-table tournaments with ten players that are similar to satellites. First place pays $500, second place pays $300, and third place pays $200. Instead of a winner-take-all deal, these online events are mini-tournaments with a much flatter payoff structure than can be found in on-land casinos. This type of structure eliminates the need for negotiating a deal at the end, as is so common in winner-take-all events at on-land casinos.

Every summer PokerStars.com offers The World Series of Online Poker, which is a series of very large tournaments that range from $109 to $1,050 to enter. The site offers super satellites for these tournaments in which you receive $1,500 in chips and play to the end without negotiating a deal. These super satellites, which have a smaller buy-in than you would normally expect to post at an on-land casino, generate multiple seats in the main tournaments.

Another difference between online and on-land events is that when your online table breaks down, you are instantaneously moved to a new table. In most on-land casinos, it takes about three minutes to physically move your body and your chips from one table to another. You save time online and thus are able to see more hands. And one other thing: Many online casinos start requiring an ante at the $100/$200 level of their no-limit hold'em satellites. On-land casinos do not require antes in their satellites; they only use them in their tournaments.

Competition

Generally, the overall quality of play is weaker in online casinos than in on-land casinos. One reason for this is that more players are using online casinos to learn how to play no-limit hold'em these days. They use the internet as a place to practice their tournament skills, which isn't a bad idea, since they'll get to play with a wide variety of people from all over the world that they've never played with before.

For instance, European players tend to play no-fear poker and put in their chips with what some of us might think are strange hands. They aren't afraid to push in the chips, and opponents like that are dangerous in no-limit hold'em, because figuring out where they're at on a hand is so difficult. For this reason, they can push you around a little bit with their fearless and aggressive style of play.

"Since I've been playing online," Brad says, "I think that my play against the Europeans has improved a lot. They used to throw me off a lot of times, but now that I've been playing against them online, I have learned how to adjust to their unique style of play. I've learned to play more cautiously against them, since it is so difficult to put them on a hand"

Strategy Tips for Playing Multi-Table No-Limit Hold'em Satellites Online

Strictly speaking, online multi-table satellites are not super satellites. They usually have four or more tables and give away as many seats for the main event as the cash in the prize pool allows. But playing multi-table satellites online is similar to playing super satellites on-land. There might be 100 to 150 people playing in a multi-table satellite with up to twenty seats being given away. Your goal is simply to win a seat, as it is in super satellites on-land. In the first levels, you play solid, waiting for other people to make mistakes. Hopefully you can pick up a hand and double up in the first one or two rounds or play a speculative hand cheaply. Since more chips are in play online, you can play a few more speculative hands in the early rounds without it costing you too much. You hope to strengthen your position a lot without hurting your chip position very much. This is particularly true in no-limit hold'em satellites, where you have big implied odds. Starting with $1,500 in chips and fifteen-minute rounds online, you have a fair amount of play and more opportunities to trap an opponent. In other words, if you limp in with a weaker type of hand, you're likely to get paid off very well if you connect with the flop—thanks to the implied odds.

The blinds usually begin at $10/$20 and increase to $15/$30, $25/$50 and $50/$100. With cautious play and occasional speculation, you have an excellent chance of surviving through the break. You don't need to get out of line to double up. If you can pick up one hand and double up with it, you probably will have $3,000 in chips, which is usually the tournament average once half the players are gone. That's a good spot to be in.

Usually, about half of the starting field is eliminated during the first hour of play. Then you take a five-minute break and when you return, the blinds increase to $75/$150. Then the blinds rise to $100/$200 for two rounds. At the beginning of the second round of $100/$200 blinds, many online casinos require you to start putting in an ante ,unlike on-land casinos, which do not require antes in satellites.

"I've found that the key to survival is knowing when you're in trouble," Brad says. "When the limits rise to $100/$200, you're at the start of crunch time. And when they rise to $200/$400, you are in the middle of crunch time."

As the limits rise, you have to start opening

up your hand requirements a little bit. You are in trouble unless you have an average amount of chips, so you must accumulate chips. This is when you change your style of play from being very solid to being more aggressive. Of course, aggressive play can pay off in any satellite you play, whether on-land or online.

"If you don't have a strong right arm, if you aren't willing to push your chips in," Tom adds, "your chances of success are greatly reduced."

At the end of the first hour, about a half of the players are gone. By the time the blinds rise to $200/$400, only about 25 percent of the players are left, and you need to have $4,000 to $5,000—about five to six times the size of the big blind—to feel secure. If you have any less than that, you will be in a move-in mode any time you play a hand. When you're in that situation, there is a good argument to be made for just moving in rather than raising $1,200 to $1,600, or three to four times the size of the blind. If you don't put in all your chips, your opponents may think that you're not fully committed and might call with marginal hands. When you move in before the flop, your opponents know that you are committed to the end, and they usually will fold those marginal hands, which is what you want them to do. Just winning the blinds is critically important at this stage. But remember, this move-in strategy applies to those times when you are short-stacked, not when you have a medium to large stack.

How Do You Know When You're in Trouble, and What Can You Do About It?

You need to know when you're in trouble, when it's time to start moving in because it's crunch time. When the blinds are at $100/$200, and especially when they rise to $200/$400, you will be in trouble if you haven't accumulated enough chips. If you have $1,000 or less at the $100/$200 level, it's probably time to start your move-in strategy. You might even consider moving in with $1,500 or less—in other words, any time you have only six to seven times the big blind, consider moving in, and when you have only five times the big blind, definitely move in.

If you have a lot of chips, you would not move all-in. You would make the standard raise because, even if you lose the pot, you will still have enough chips to play another hand. Further, you have the option of folding if you need to. But when you're short-stacked, you don't have many options; you simply have to play a hand all the way once you start and hope that you can double through if you get called.

At the $200/$400 level with a $50 ante, it's move-in time if you have $2,500 or less. If you have $3,000 to $4,000, you can make a standard raise, but you still are pretty well committed to going the rest of the way. Remember that any time you have half of your chips in the pot, you are pretty much committed. At the $300/$600 level, you usually will be moving in if you have $3,000 to $4,500 because of the double-whammy impact of the blinds plus the ante. Once the antes come into the mix, you need to have more than seven to eight times the size of the big blind to feel comfortable.

One question to ask yourself that will help you make a decision as to whether you should call a player who has reraised you is, "What are my chances of coming back if I give up the chips that I raised with?" Also keep tabs on other players who are in trouble at your table, and who you can steal the blinds from. We hope this explanation of how to know when you're in trouble and what to do about it will help you design your strategy for your online satellite play.

How Many Chips Per Round Does It Take to Play in Online Multi-Table Satellites?

Figure out what it will cost you to play each round. For example, when the satellite gets to the seventh level, you're playing $100/$200 blinds with a $25 ante. It costs $525 per round to play. At the next level, the blinds are $200/$400 with $25 antes, meaning that it costs $825 per round. If you have $1,650 at the start of the $200/$400, you will go broke in two rounds if you don't play a hand. At the $300/$600 level with a $50 ante, it will cost you $1,350 to play each round. At $400/$800 with a $50 ante, you will need $1,650 to play one round. When the blinds rise to $600/$1,200, the ante rises to $75 so it will cost you $2,475 per round. At $1,000/$2,000 with a $100 ante, you will need $3,900 to play one round. These examples assume that you have nine players at your table.

The amount of chips it will cost you to play a round is always a factor in your strategy, since it affects your opening-hand requirements. You cannot afford to sit there and let yourself get blinded and anted out of action. When you only have enough chips to go through the blinds and antes two times, you are hanging on by your fingernails. If you have any less than that, you are in an even worse position. The problem with letting your chip count fall too low is that your opponents usually are going to play with you with a lot of marginal hands, so you need to do whatever it takes to prevent your stack from getting too low. In fact one big-name player said that he would rather go all-in without even looking at his hand than allow himself to be blinded and anted out of action.

"When your chip count falls to two and a half to three times the amount that it costs you to play a round, it's really crunch time," Brad says. "At that point, if you take the blinds, you won't have enough money to blow anybody out."

When you get that short on chips, you won't have enough chips to put any significant pressure on your opponents, and they are going to call you. For this reason, you're going to have to move your chips in before you get to that point.

Suppose you have only enough chips to play two rounds. You pick up a hand that you want to play, but someone beats you into the pot. Here you were all set to move your chips in and the mean guy sitting to your right moves first. His aggressive play has shut you out of the pot. Unless you have a hand that is good enough to take a stand with, there is very little you can do in this scenario except grit your teeth and wait for a better spot. You want a situation where you can be the first player in the pot, put in your chips, and win it uncontested. Sometimes this means that you will have to raise from right up front with a hand that you figure to be better than a random blind hand and take a shot with it—even K-Q, K-J, or A-10.

However if you are extremely short on chips and you don't get any kind of a decent hand to go all-in with, you might be just as well off taking the big blind and playing it in the dark. Some players will get desperate and play a really substandard hand when they're one or two spots in front of the big blind. But they are forgetting that they have to run the gauntlet, so to speak, by getting through all the players yet to act behind them. They don't realize that they often would be better off taking the big blind.

"There is some power in taking the blind when you're very short on chips," Brad adds. "Your opponents know that you are pot-committed, they know you have to play any two cards. For this reason, they sometimes will lay down a medium-strength hand from early position because they're afraid that somebody will raise from a later position."

For example, suppose an aggressive player sitting in an early position picks up a hand that he might ordinarily raise with coming into the pot. Since he knows that you're going to play the hand no matter what happens and since he is leery of running into a better hand behind him, he may back off. In other words, when you're committed to the pot, your opponents cannot make as many plays against you. Tournament pro An Tran is famous for saying, "Look, boos, no-look poker!" Translation: "I'm calling you in the dark."

You cannot manufacture a good hand. Chip count and positional considerations separate the men from the boys, so to speak. Making the right decisions about when to move, when to push the panic button, and when to be patient are important parts of the game. Just because you're short-chipped and have only enough for two more rounds, that doesn't necessarily mean that you should push the panic button. Sometimes you just have to wait and take advantage of your best opportunity.

"One of the things I wrote in *Tournament Poker* is that you have to last long enough to give yourself a chance to get lucky," Tom explains. "Whoever wins a tournament or a satellite has gotten lucky along the way. But you can't get lucky if you're no longer in it. You must develop good survival skills. You need to know when to move with your marginal hands with short to medium stacks, for example. And in satellites, you will be playing a short stack frequently."

In fact playing short-stacked is the norm rather than the exception in satellite play. Knowing when you're committed, when you have to go with a hand, and learning how to fire your way out of getting too short are important survival skills to master.

Strategy Tips for Playing Multi-Table Limit Hold'em Satellites Online

You won't find nearly as many multi-table online satellites for limit hold'em as you will for no-limit hold'em, because no-limit hold'em is the game that is played in the championship event of most of the major tournaments, online and on-land. However some tournaments feature a big buy-in limit hold'em tournament. The PartyPoker Million cruise tournament features a big limit hold'em championship event, and PokerStars.com also offers a big limit hold'em event for which they spread multi-table satellites.

The biggest difference between playing a limit hold'em and a no-limit hold'em satellite is that in limit play, you usually will have to show the best hand. In other words, you usually will be called in most pots. In a typical limit satellite, you receive $1,500 in chips and start off playing with $10/$20 blinds and $20/$40 limits. Then it goes to $15/$30 blinds, $30/$60 limits; $25/$50 blinds, $50/$100 limits; and so on. Unlike no-limit satellites, there are no antes. Sometimes the blinds double at the beginning of each new round but usually not, and at some sites, you start with $1,000 in chips and play a fixed number of hands before the blinds rise.

Given the number of chips you start with and the low limits, the first few rounds are not as important as the later rounds. If you win a hand, it won't help you that much, and if you lose a hand, it won't hurt you a lot. Generally, you will be playing solid poker.

"But I don't mind playing a few more speculative hands in the early rounds when the blinds are low and I can come in cheaply from late position," Tom says. "I want to have a couple of limpers already in the pot before I play suited connectors or small pairs, so I will be getting a good price for the hand."

However if you blow off a lot of chips by playing too many speculative hands, you will decrease your chances of winning. You're simply looking for situations where you can accumulate some chips without risking a lot, so that it won't hurt your position too much if you lose. It wouldn't hurt too badly, in fact, if you didn't even play the first couple of rounds in these online multi-table satellites. If all you do is pay the blinds, you still wouldn't be very short on chips. This is not true of on-land satellites where you start with a lot fewer chips.

Once the limits rise to $50/$100 and $100/$200, it is very important that you get out there and play. Your chip position can deteriorate at these levels if you never play a hand because it costs you $75 to $150 per round to play. In these early rounds, you want to create a table image, study your opponents to see how they're playing, survive, and try to add chips to your stack without seriously jeopardizing it. You try to hold even, tread water a little bit to maintain your position.

From the fourth level onward, the chips will start to get distributed more quickly, with bigger blinds and higher limits. We do not advocate playing trash hands at these limits, but you should be looking for situations where you can be the aggressor. Look for spots where you have position and can be the first one in the pot. Determine which players are more liberal blind defenders and which are tighter and can be run over more easily. If you have a marginal hand that you want to play and you are in position, just remember that most of the time you will get called and have to go to the showdown. For this reason, you cannot expect to run over people just because you have position on them.

In limit hold'em satellites you will see more multiway pots than in no-limit hold'em, especially during the first few levels of play. As players get eliminated and the limits rise, fewer multiway pots will be played. Most of the pots at the higher limits will be three-handed or heads-up.

You will see the chips of the very aggressive players fluctuating widely, even in the early rounds. They accumulate a lot of chips, and sometimes they'll get very short and make a comeback with their aggressive play. Their opponents get accustomed to their style in the early rounds. Then when the limits get high, it's easy for the aggressive player to get lots of action. His opponents start following suit, firing in their chips and going after him, so that he has the opportunity to win even more chips.

When you have an aggressive image and put constant pressure on your opponents, they know that they will need to have a hand to take a stand against you. Usually, the aggressive player will not back off even if he gets reraised. This is another advantage of having an aggressive image in satellite play. Since you're always putting pressure on the pot, your opponents often will not call you with a hand that they might have called you with in a live-action game.

Aggressive players have an advantage over conservative players—they have a better idea of where the cautious players are at in a hand than conservative players have of where aggressive opponents are at in the hand. Good, aggressive players develop a feel for what their opponents have. They know that if they are called by a tight player, he usually has a premium hand. The aggressive player is harder to read because he's in so many pots, and it's difficult to always tell how strong he is. But when a player who is very selective about his hands comes into a pot, it is easier to eliminate the types of hands that he will not play and, thus, put him on a hand.

How Do You Know When You're in Trouble, and What Can You Do About It?

Any time that you cannot play two hands through to the river with at least one bet on every street, you are short on chips. This doesn't include having enough to call raises. What can you do to improve your chip position when you get short on chips? Suppose you have $300 to $400 and the blinds are \$50/\$100. If you enter the pot, bring it in for a raise. If you have half your chips in the pot, realize that you are pot-committed and will be going all the way with the hand. If you simply cannot find a playable hand when you are that short on chips—and you know that you will get played with—wait for the blinds. The idea is to give yourself the opportunity to look at as many hands as possible before you enter the pot.

One of the major differences between no-limit and limit hold'em is that in limit hold'em you cannot protect your hand or possibly win without much of a hand by moving all-in. You will get called in limit hold'em, and the shorter you are, the more likely your opponents will look you up. But like no-limit play, if your opponents notice that you are so short that you're committed to the pot no matter what happens, they might give you a little more respect because they don't want to take the chance of doubling you up.

When you're really short, you might take a shot with a hand such as pocket sevens or eights. Even if two overcards come on the flop, as long as one of them is not an ace, you most likely will continue playing anyway, although you won't like it very much. There's always the chance that your pair is the best hand, since a lot of people will play hands such as ace-rag against a short stack. Say that the flop comes K-Q-4 and you have pocket eights. If you only have two bets left in your stack, you may very well commit. The reasoning is that you will have to win a hand, or you will be out of the satellite. It's almost damned-if-you-do and damned-if-you-don't. If you don't put in your chips, you're crippled anyway. And if you aren't beaten, you might as well milk the hand for all its worth, even though it looks dangerous. Also, if you are first to bet, you are giving your opponent a chance to throw his hand away.

Now, let's say that you have $300 in chips, and the blinds are $50/$100. You are the big blind and look down at pocket sevens. An opponent raises to $200 from late position. What's your move?

It depends. Sometimes you will raise your last $100. Other times you will just call save the $100 in chips, and then bet your last $100 on the flop, giving your opponent the opportunity to throw away his hand. This is one of the advantages of saving your last bet until the flop. There are even times when you might get someone to lay down a better hand by betting on the flop. Say that the flop comes K-8-3. You have pocket sevens, and your opponent has pocket jacks. You bet your last $100 into him on the flop. He may give you credit for having a king in your hand and fold. So sometimes, saving that last $100 to bet is a good thing to do.

The types of hands with which you would be more likely to throw in your final chip are big connectors, such as A-K or A-Q. You know that you will see all the flop cards, no matter what comes.

On the other hand, suppose you have a lot of chips and notice that an opponent is short-stacked. You need to take into account how you think he's going to play his hand, especially if he is in the big blind. There are a lot of hands that he will play if he has only $100 left. You want to have a better than average hand if you're going to raise in this situation, because you know the chances are good that he's going to play with you. You don't want to double up a short stack with an inferior hand. But if you have a little bit better hand—such as a pair, two cards 10 or higher, or ace-anything—you might consider attacking his blind because your hand figures to be better than his random blind hand.

Now suppose it's down to you in the $50 small blind against the big blind. You have plenty of chips, but the player in the $100 big blind has only $100 left in his stack. You look down and find J-10. What play will give you the best chance to win the pot? Smooth-call the $50 and then bet the flop, no matter what comes. Why? Because the big blind has half of his chips in on the blind, and he most likely would have called if you had raised before the flop. When you just smooth-call and then bet into him after the flop, you're giving him a chance to fold his hand so that you can win the pot.

Playing When You Have a Medium Stack

A medium stack, one with enough chips to play three or four hands to the river, may be the most difficult size stack to play. If you have a medium stack, the big stacks have to be leery of getting too involved against you—especially in raised pots—because if you double through a big stack, you will become a big stack yourself, and the big stack will be reduced to a medium stack. In the same way, a medium stack has to play more carefully against a short stack to try to prevent the short stack from doubling through and becoming a medium stack, thus reducing the medium stack to a short stack.

You have to make tricky decisions more often when you have a medium stack than you do when you have a short stack or a big stack. Playing a medium stack requires a lot of judgment: A wrong decision at the wrong level can seriously hamper your chances of winning a tournament seat. Conversely, making the right play at the right time can tremendously increase your chances of winning a seat. With a medium stack, you must be far more selective about the hands you play and who you play them against.

As the limits get higher, a limit hold'em satellite takes on a lot of the qualities of a no-limit hold'em satellite. For all practical purposes, when you have only enough chips left to play one hand to the river, you are playing no-limit hold'em because you can only go to the river one time. If you have enough chips to play three or four hands to the river, winning or losing one of those hands can drastically affect your chip status. You can become a big stack if you win, or a short stack if you lose.

Playing a Big Stack

When you have a big stack—which, unfortunately, is the exception rather than the rule—you must consider several factors. First, you want to protect and add to your stack. You don't want to jeopardize your chips by playing marginal hands, especially against shorter stacks who most likely will be forced to play with you to the river because of their inferior chip position. If a player in the big blind already has a third to a half of his chips in the pot, he will be forced to play with you if you attack him. Therefore, you don't want to attack him with hands such as 10-9. You want to have a better hand because you figure that you will have to show down the best hand at the end. You do not want to play a marginal hand against a medium stack, either, because if you lose one hand to him, you may wind up as a medium stack yourself. Furthermore, you may help create a monster if the medium stack doubles through you.

When you have the chip lead, you always want

to start with the best hand if you can. You want to preserve and protect. Looking at your opponents, determine who is committed, who is going to go all the way with a hand, and who is likely to give it up. If an opponent is very aggressive, you may simply check-call, check-call, in order to protect your chips. Your goal is to either win the maximum or lose the minimum. Very often the correct play against an aggressive opponent is the check-call.

A-K Scenario One

Now, suppose you are in the small blind with a big stack. Two limpers have entered the pot, and you look down at A-K. Since A-K is a drawing hand, your best play may be to just flat-call and wait to see the flop. If you flop something, you can either bet or try for a check-raise. Quite often your opponents will not give you credit for having such a big hand, and you will be able to add some chips to your stack by either breaking or crippling an opponent. And if you flop nothing, you can get away from the hand cheaply. Always remember that a bet saved is just as important as a bet earned—especially in a satellite, because that saved bet can help you survive longer.

If the flop comes 5-3-2 or three other random little cards, your opponents know that you can have anything. Most likely, they probably don't have a pocket pair or they would have brought it in for a raise. In this case, you might be able to pick up the pot on the flop. Or suppose it comes 9-3-3, for example. If you bet on the flop, they may think that it's quite possible that you have a 9 or even a 3 in your hand since you just called before the flop. The point is that when you are playing against a short to medium stack, you can add a lot of deception to your game by not raising from the blind with hands like A-K before the flop,.

A-K Scenario Two

What if you are sitting in early position with A-K and a medium stack, when the big blind has a short stack and the small blind has a big stack? How do you play it in this situation? You will bring it in for a raise if you are the first one in the pot. Even if you expect to get played with by the big blind, you most likely have the best starting hand, and you also have position over him. Your raise also gives the small blind—the guy you least want to play against—food for thought. "Here's a medium stack raising under the gun," he might think. "I'd better watch out." He may still play the hand, but at least you will have slowed him down a bit.

A-K Scenario Three

Let's say that a player with a short stack brings it in for a raise, and a medium stack three-bets the pot. The short stack has one and a half bets left in his stack. You are sitting in the big blind with a big stack and an A-K. What is your best move? In this scenario, you realize that the medium stack probably is trying blast everyone else out of the pot to get heads-up with the short stack. So, you might decide to get in his way by calling the reraise. Your call weakens the medium stack's hand. He knows the short stack is going to play with him, and now he has a second opponent. Always remember that there are many factors to consider in playing a hand, and often, there is more than one correct way to play each hand.

Two Vintage
Satellite Stories

11

In the early days, satellites were not always taken as seriously as they are today. Here are two classic satellite stories from years past.

From Brad Daugherty

In 1987 Tuna Lund and I were in Las Vegas and heard that the Gold Coast was holding a satellite for the $10,000 championship event at the WSOP. We had been planning to ride our motorcycles out in the hills that day, but decided to check out the Gold Coast action first.

When we arrived in the poker room, we ran into Mike Sexton, currently the play-by-play commentator for the World Poker Tour, and told him we hadn't decided yet whether to ride or play.

"I tell ya what, guys," Mike said. "Since you're thinking about riding your bikes, why don't I just buy lunch for you and give you some gasoline money so as to make it a real nice day for the two of you?"

Sounded to us like Mike kinda wanted to buy us off to get us outta there so he'd have a better chance. We debated his kind offer, but decided to play the satellite instead of taking a ride. Tuna finished first, and I came second. That was the first super satellite I'd ever played—and it was the last time the Fish ever beat me heads-up.

From *Cowboys, Gamblers & Hustlers* by Cowboy Wolford

In his book *Cowboys, Gamblers & Hustlers*, the late Cowboy Wolford told the following story about a "titanic" satellite that was held during the early 1970s. It seems that a couple of players were shooting the bull with Titanic Thompson at the World Series of Poker.

"Ty, do you think you could win this World Series?" they asked.

"Hell, yeah," he boasted. "Nobody can beat me playing poker. Of course I'm getting at the age where I can't play for no fifteen hours like I used to, but if it wasn't for that, I probably could be the world champion every year."

"Well, why don't you play in one of them satellites?" someone suggested. "You'll only have to play for a couple of hours and if you win the chips, we'll make a deal where you can cash them out and you won't have to play in the big tournament."

Ty told them he might go for the deal later and left.

He walked straight out into the casino, found nine players, and gave each one of them an entry fee into the satellite plus an extra $300 to dump the money off to him. They could play legitimately against each other if Ty wasn't in the pot, but if he was in it, they'd push the money to him.

Then he rejoined the men he had been talking with earlier and said, "I've been watching one of them satellites, and they can't play worth a damn. I sure wish I could last fifteen hours in a big tournament 'cause I know I could beat 'em."

They all were laughing at his big brag.

"I'll play one of them satellites if I can get the right price, but if I have to play for more than three hours, win or lose, it's no bet."

They all knew the satellites didn't last for three hours, so they agreed. In the early days, the satellites weren't as popular as they are now, so people weren't standing in long lines to play them like they have to do these days.

When they got to the satellite area, Ty announced, "Come on, boys, let's get us a satellite going. I've got a little bet on it."

One by one, the nine shills started signing up for the game.

"We've got a satellite table put together," Ty told the group of bettors, "so now let's settle on a price."

Sid Bernstein and a few other famous gamblers finally agreed on 5 to 1 odds. And hell, they were betting something—$1,500, $2,500, $3,000—so Ty ended up with about a $10,000 bet on it.

To make a long story short, Ty won the satellite. The bettors were in shock. And all the shills were happy as pie because they'd just made a score for themselves, not knowing how much Ty had made off the deal.

"I told you I could beat all these sonnabitches," he bragged once again. "They just can't play as good as I can."

And that's how, even as a very old man, Titanic Thompson took 'em off for a whole lot of money at the World Series of Poker.

Satellite Terminology

Add-on: A stack of chips that players have the option to buy at the end of the rebuy period in a tournament. This is the last opportunity players have to buy chips in a rebuy event.

Backer: Someone who pays the entry fees for a tournament player with whom he will split the rewards.

Buy-in: The money that you pay to enter a tournament, for which all players receive a fixed number of chips.

Case chips: A player's last chips.

Change gears: To change your style of play from aggressive to passive, from tight to loose, or from fast to slow to adjust to changing table conditions.

Chip status: How the number of chips that you have in front of you compares to those of your opponents.

Come over the top: Reraise your opponent.

Commit: To put all your remaining chips in the pot, knowing you will be there until the end.

Confrontation: A heads-up showdown between two players over a big pot that often significantly changes the chip status of the opponents or alters the outcome of the tournament.

Double through: To win a pot and double your number of chips.

Get full value: To bet, raise, and reraise in order to manipulate the size of the pot so that you will get maximum pot odds if you win the hand.

Get the right price: To be in a position to continue playing the hand since the pot is laying you the correct odds to do so.

Lay down a hand: To fold to a bet or a raise.

Level: The current round of play in the satellite, such as Level 2 with $25/$50 blinds or Level 3 with $50/$100 blinds.

Limp in: To enter the pot by calling rather than raising another player's bet. A limper is a player who has entered the pot by just calling the minimum opening bet.

Make a deal: To negotiate a new way of dividing the chips or money among the top finishers at the last table in a satellite.

Make a move: To execute a calculated play to try to improve your chip position, sometimes a bluff.

Maniac: A very aggressive player who often plays hands that solid or conservative players would not consider.

Multi-Table Satellite: A satellite in which there is more than one starting table, such as a super satellite.

Nuts: The best possible hand.

Online Satellite: A satellite played in cyberspace on the Internet.

On-Land Satellite: A satellite played live, usually in a casino.

One-Table Satellite: A satellite that has one table only, usually with nine or ten players.

Out: A card that will make your hand.

Payout: The prize money you win at the end of the event.

Play back: To respond to an opponent's bet by raising or reraising.

Play fast: To aggressively bet a drawing hand to get full value for it if you make it.

Play with: 1. To participate in the hand; 2. to call someone's bet.

Rag: A board card that doesn't help you.

Read: To determine what your opponent is holding or the significance of his betting strategy.

Rebuy: The amount of money that you pay to add a fixed number of chips to your stack in a tournament.

Rebuy period: The time frame within which you are allowed to make a rebuy in a tournament, usually the first three rounds.

Ring game: Not a tournament game; a cash game.

Rise: The increase in chips that it takes to post the blinds or antes at the start of a new round in a satellite. If the blinds rise from $10/$20 to $20/$40, the blinds have doubled.

Rock: A very conservative player who always waits for premium cards before he plays a hand.

Round: The predetermined length of time that each betting increment is in force during a tournament (twenty minutes, one hour, and so on).

Run over: To play aggressively in an attempt to control the responses of your opponents.

Solid player: An accomplished player who employs optimal strategy at all times.

Satellite: A feeder tournament in which you can win an entry into the major tournament for a fraction of its cost.

Super Satellite: A rebuy, multi-table feeder tournament that awards several seats into the championship event of the main tournament.

Stack: A pile of chips.

Stack-off: To move in all your chips.

Survival: Playing conservatively rather than betting for maximum value in an attempt to last longer in the tournament.

Tell: A physical mannerism that a player consistently exhibits at the table which enables his opponents to determine what he is holding or what he is likely to do during the play of a hand.

Vigorish: The fee that casinos charge to players to cover house expenses. The "vig" is added to the buy-in for a satellite tournament.

Wake up with a hand: To be dealt a premium hand, such as two aces or two kings, in hold'em.

Where you're at: The value of your hand compared to your opponent's hand.

THE CHAMPIONSHIP SERIES
POWERFUL BOOKS YOU MUST HAVE

CHAMPIONSHIP TOURNAMENT POKER by Tom McEvoy. New Cardoza Edition! Rated by pros as best book on tournaments ever written and enthusiastically endorsed by more than five world champions, this is the definitive guide to winning tournaments and a must for every player's library. McEvoy lets you in on the secrets he has used to win millions of dollars in tournaments and the insights he has learned competing against the best players in the world. Packed solid with winning strategies for all 11 games in the World Series of Poker, with extensive discussions of 7-card stud, limit hold'em, pot and no-limit hold'em, Omaha high-low, re-buy, half-half tournaments, satellites, and strategies for each stage of tournaments. Tons of essential concepts and specific strategies jam-pack the book. Phil Hellmuth, 1989 WSOP champion says, "[this] is the world's most definitive guide to winning poker tournaments." 416 pages, paperback, $29.95.

CHAMPIONSHIP TABLE (at the World Series of Poker) by Dana Smith, Ralph Wheeler, and Tom McEvoy. New Cardoza Edition! From 1970 when the champion was presented a silver cup, to the present when the champion was awarded more than $2 million, *Championship Table* celebrates three decades of poker greats who have competed to win poker's most coveted title. This book gives you the names and photographs of all the players who made the final table, pictures of the last hand the champion played against the runner-up, how they played their cards, and how much they won. This book also features fascinating interviews and conversations with the champions and runners-up and interesting highlights from each Series. This is a fascinating and invaluable resource book for WSOP and gaming buffs. In some cases the champion himself wrote "how it happened," as did two-time champion Doyle Brunson when Stu Ungar caught a wheel in 1980 on the turn to deprive "Texas Dolly" of his third title. Includes tons of vintage photographs. 208 pages, paperback, $19.95.

WIN YOUR WAY INTO BIG MONEY HOLD'EM TOURNAMENTS: CHAMPIONSHIP SERIES by Brad Daugherty & Tom McEvoy. In 2002 and 2003, satellite players won their way into the $10,000 WSOP buy-in and emerged as champions, winning more than $2 million each. You can too! You'll learn specific, proven strategies for winning almost any satellite. Learn the ten ways to win a seat at the WSOP and other big tournaments, how to win limit hold'em and no-limit hold'em satellites, one-table satellites for big tournaments, and online satellites, plus how to play the final table of super satellites. McEvoy and Daugherty sincerely believe that if you practice these strategies, you can win your way into any tournament for a fraction of the buy-in. You'll learn how much to bet, how hard to pressure opponents, how to tell when an opponent is bluffing, how to play deceptively, and how to use your chips as weapons of destruction. Includes a special chapter on no-limit hold'em satellites! 320 pages. Illustrated, glossary. $29.95.

CHAMPIONSHIP HOLD'EM TOURNAMENT HANDS by T.J. Cloutier & Tom McEvoy. Two tournament legends show you how to become a winning tournament player. Get inside their heads as they think their way through the correct strategy at 57 limit and no-limit practice hands. Cloutier and McEvoy show you how to use your skill and intuition to play strategic hands for maximum profit in real tournament scenarios and how 45 key hands were played by champions in turnaround situations at the WSOP. By sharing their analysis on how the winners and losers played key hands, you'll gain tremendous insights into how tournament poker is played at the highest levels. Learn how champions think and how they play major hands in strategic tournament situations, Cloutier and McEvoy believe that you will be able to win your share of the profits in today's tournaments—and join them at the championship table far sooner than you ever imagined. 368 pages, illustrated with card pictures, $29.95

THE CHAMPIONSHIP SERIES
POWERFUL BOOKS YOU MUST HAVE

CHAMPIONSHIP HOLD'EM by Tom McEvoy & T.J. Cloutier. Hard-hitting hold'em the way it's played today in both limit cash games and tournaments. Get killer advice on how to win more money in rammin'-jammin' games, kill-pot, jackpot, shorthanded, and other types of cash games. You'll learn the thinking process before the flop, on the flop, on the turn, and at the river with specific suggestions for what to do when good or bad things happen plus 20 illustrated hands with play-by-play analyses. Specific advice for rocks in tight games, weaklings in loose games, experts in solid games, how hand values change in jackpot games, when you should fold, check, raise, reraise, check-raise, slowplay, bluff, and tournament strategies for small buy-in, big buy-in, rebuy, incremental add-on, satellite and big-field major tournaments. Wow! Easy-to-read and conversational, if you want to become a lifelong winner at limit hold'em, you need this book! 388 Pages, Illustrated, Photos. ~~$39.95~~. Now only $29.95!

CHAMPIONSHIP NO-LIMIT & POT-LIMIT HOLD'EM by T.J. Cloutier & Tom McEvoy. New Cardoza Edition! The definitive guide to winning at two of the world's most exciting poker games! Written by eight time World Champion players T.J. Cloutier (1998 and 2002 Player of the Year) and Tom McEvoy (the foremost author on tournament strategy) who have won millions of dollars each playing no-limit and pot-limit hold'em in cash games and major tournaments around the world. You'll get all the answers here—no holds barred—to your most important questions: How do you get inside your opponents' heads and learn how to beat them at their own game? How can you tell how much to bet, raise, and reraise in no-limit hold'em? When can you bluff? How do you set up your opponents in pot-limit hold'em so you can win a monster pot? What are the best strategies for winning no-limit and pot-limit tournaments, satellites, and supersatellites? You get rock-solid and inspired advice from two of the most recognizable figures in poker—advice that you can bank on. If you want to become a winning player, and a champion, you must have this book. 304 pages, paperback, illustrations, photos. $29.95

CHAMPIONSHIP OMAHA (Omaha High-Low, Pot-limit Omaha, Limit High Omaha) by Tom McEvoy & T.J. Cloutier. Clearly-written strategies and powerful advice from Cloutier and McEvoy who have won four World Series of Poker titles in Omaha tournaments. Powerful advice shows you how to win at low-limit and high-stakes games, how to play against loose and tight opponents, and the differing strategies for rebuy and freezeout tournaments. Learn the best starting hands, when slowplaying a big hand is dangerous, what danglers are and why winners don't play them, why pot-limit Omaha is the only poker game where you sometimes fold the nuts on the flop and are correct in doing so and overall, and how you can win a lot of money at Omaha! 230 pages, photos, illustrations, ~~$39.95~~. Now only $29.95!

CHAMPIONSHIP STUD (Seven-Card Stud, Stud 8/or Better and Razz) by Dr. Max Stern, Linda Johnson, and Tom McEvoy. The authors, who have earned millions of dollars in major tournaments and cash games, eight World Series of Poker bracelets and hundreds of other titles in competition against the best players in the world show you the winning strategies for medium-limit side games as well as poker tournaments and a general tournament strategy that is applicable to any form of poker. Includes give-and-take conversations between the authors to give you more than one point of view on how to play poker. 200 pages, hand pictorials, photos. $39.95.

FROM CARDOZA'S EXCITING LIBRARY
ADD THESE TO YOUR COLLECTION - ORDER NOW!

COWBOYS, GAMBLERS & HUSTLERS: The True Adventures of a Rodeo Champion & Poker Legend by Byron "Cowboy" Wolford. Ride along with the road gamblers as they fade the white line from Dallas to Shreveport to Houston in the 1960s in search of a score. Feel the fear and frustration of being hijacked, getting arrested for playing poker, and having to outwit card sharps and scam artists. Wolford survived it all to win a WSOP gold bracelet playing with poker greats Amarillo Slim Preston, Johnny Moss and Bobby Baldwin (and 30 rodeo belt buckles). Read fascinating yarns about life on the rough and tumble, and colorful adventures as a road gambler and hustler gambling in smoky backrooms with legends Titanic Thompson, Jack Straus, Doyle Brunson and get a look at vintage Las Vegas when Cowboy's friend, Benny Binion ruled Glitter Gulch. Read about the most famous bluff in WSOP history. Endorsed by Jack Binion, Doyle Brunson and Bobby Baldwin, who says, Cowboy is probably the best gambling story teller in the world. 304 pages, $19.95.

SECRETS OF WINNING POKER by Tex Sheahan. This is a compilation of Sheahan's best articles from 15 years of writing for the major gaming magazines as his legacy to poker players. Sheahan gives you sound advice on winning poker strategies for hold'em and 7-card stud. Chapters on tournament play, psychology, personality profiles and some very funny stories from the greenfelt jungle. "Some of the best advice you'll ever read on how to win at poker" --Doyle Brunson. 200 pages, paperback. $19.95.

OMAHA HI-LO: Play to Win with the Odds by Bill Boston. Selecting the right hands to play is the most important decision you'll make in Omaha high-low poker. In this book you'll find the odds for every hand dealt in Omaha high-low—the chances that the hand has of winning the high end of the pot, the low end of it, and how often it is expected to scoop the whole pot. The results are based on 10,000 simulations for each one of the possible 5,211 Omaha high-low hands. Boston has organized the data into an easy-to-use format and added insights learned from years of experience. Learn the 5,211 Omaha high-low hands, the 49 best hands and their odds, the 49 worst hands, trap hands to avoid, and 30 Ace-less hands you can play for profit. A great tool for Omaha players! 156 pages, $19.95.

OMAHA HI-LO POKER (8 OR BETTER): How to win at the lower limits by Shane Smith. Since its first printing in 1991, this has become the classic in the field for low-limit players. Readers have lauded the author's clear and concise writing style. Smith shows you how to put players on hands, read the board for high and low, avoid dangerous draws, and use winning betting strategies. Chapters include starting hands, the flop, the turn, the river, and tournament strategy. Illustrated with pictorials of sample hands, an odds chart, and a starting hands chart. Lou Krieger, author of *Poker for Dummies*, says, Shane Smith's book is terrific! If you're new to Omaha high-low split or if you're a low-limit player who wants to improve your game, you ought to have this book in your poker library. Complex concepts are presented in an easy-to-understand format. It's a gem! 82 pages, spiralbound. $17.95.

THE WACKY SIDE OF POKER by Ralph E. Wheeler. Take a walk on the wacky side with 88 humorous poker cartoons! Also includes 220 wise and witty poker quotes. Lighten up from all the heavy reading and preparation of the games with a quick walk through this fun book. Perfect for a holiday gift. 176 pages filled with wit and wisdom will bring a smile to your face. At less than a ten-spot, you can't go wrong! 176 pages, $11.95.

FROM CARDOZA'S EXCITING LIBRARY
ADD THESE TO YOUR COLLECTION - ORDER NOW!

POKER WISDOM OF A CHAMPION by Doyle Brunson. Learn what it takes to be a great poker player by climbing inside the mind of poker's most famous champion. Fascinating anecdotes and adventures from Doyle's early career playing poker in roadhouses and with other great champions are interspersed with important lessons you can learn from the champion who has made more money at poker than anyone else in the history of the game. You'll learn what makes a great player tick, how he approaches the game, and receive candid, powerful advice from the legend himself. The Mad Genius of poker, Mike Caro, says, "Brunson is the greatest poker player who ever lived. This book shows why." 192 pages. $14.95.

CARO'S BOOK OF POKER TELLS by Mike Caro. The classic book is now revised and back in print! This long-awaited brand new edition by the Mad Genius of Poker, takes a detailed look at the art and science of tells, the physical giveaways by players on their hands. Featuring photos of poker players in action along with Caro's explanations about when players are bluffing and when they're not. These powerful eye-opening ideas can give you the decisive edge at the table! This invaluable book should be in every player's library! 320 pages. $24.95.

KEN WARREN TEACHES TEXAS HOLD'EM by Ken Warren. This is a step-by-step comprehensive manual for making money at hold'em poker. 42 powerful chapters will teach you one lesson at a time. Great practical advice and concepts with examples from actual games and how to apply them to your own play. Lessons include: Starting Cards, Playing Position, Which Hands to Play, Raising, Check-raising, Tells, Game/Seat Selection, Dominated Hands, Odds, and much more. This book is already a huge fan favorite and best-seller! 416 pages. $26.95.

WINNERS GUIDE TO TEXAS HOLD'EM POKER by Ken Warren. The most powerful book on beating hold'em shows serious players how to play every hand from every position with every type of flop. Learn the 14 categories of starting hands, the 10 most common hold'em tells, how to evaluate a game for profit, value of deception, art of bluffing, eight secrets to winning, starting hand categories, position, and more! Bonus: Includes detailed analysis of the top 40 hands and the most complete chapter on hold'em odds in print. Over 500,000 copies in print. 224 pages. $16.95.

THE BIG BOOK OF POKER by Ken Warren. This easy-to-read and oversized guide teaches you everything you need to know to win money at home poker, in cardrooms, casinos and on the tournament circuit. Readers will learn how to bet, raise, and checkraise, bluff, semi-bluff, and how to take advantage of position and pot odds. Great sections on hold'em (plus, stud games, Omaha, draw games, and many more) and playing and winning poker on the internet. Packed with charts, diagrams, sidebars, and detailed, easy-to-read examples by best-selling poker expert Ken Warren, this wonderfully formatted book is one stop shopping for players ready to take on any form of poker for real money. Want to be a big player? Buy the *Big Book of Poker*! 320 oversized pages. $19.95.

HOW TO PLAY WINNING POKER by Avery Cardoza. New and expanded edition shows playing and winning strategies for all major games: 5 and 7-stud games, Omaha, draw poker, hold'em, and high-low, both for home and casino play. You'll learn 15 winning poker concepts, how to minimize losses and maximize profits, how to read opponents and gain the edge against their style, how to use use pot odds, tells, position, more. 160 pages. $12.95.

POWERFUL POKER SIMULATIONS
A MUST FOR SERIOUS PLAYERS WITH A COMPUTER!
IBM compatibles CD ROM Win 95, 98, 2000, NT, ME, XP - Full Color Graphics

These **incredible** full color poker simulation programs are the absolute **best** method to improve your game. Computer opponents play like real players. All games let you set the limits and rake, have fully programmable players, adjustable lineup, stat tracking, and Hand Analyzer for starting hands. Mike Caro, the world's foremost poker theoretician says, "Amazing...a steal for under $500...get it, it's great." Includes free telephone support. "Smart Advisor" gives expert advice for every play in every game!

1. TURBO TEXAS HOLD'EM FOR WINDOWS - $89.95 - Choose which players, how many, 2-10, you want to play, create loose/tight game, control check-raising, bluffing, position, sensitivity to pot odds, more! Also, instant replay, pop-up odds, Professional Advisor, keeps track of play statistics. Free bonus: Hold'em Hand Analyzer analyzes all 169 pocket hands in detail, their win rates under any conditions you set. Caro says this "hold'em software is the most powerful ever created." Great product!

2. TURBO SEVEN-CARD STUD FOR WINDOWS - $89.95 - Create any conditions of play; choose number of players (2-8), bet amounts, fixed or spread limit, bring-in method, tight/loose conditions, position, reaction to board, number of dead cards, stack deck to create special conditions, instant replay. Terrific stat reporting includes analysis of starting cards, 3-D bar charts, graphs. Play interactively, run high speed simulation to test strategies. Hand Analyzer analyzes starting hands in detail. Wow!

3. TURBO OMAHA HIGH-LOW SPLIT FOR WINDOWS - $89.95 -Specify any playing conditions; betting limits, number of raises, blind structures, button position, aggressiveness/passiveness of opponents, number of players (2-10), types of hands dealt, blinds, position, board reaction, specify flop, turn, river cards! Choose opponents, use provided point count or create your own. Statistical reporting, instant replay, pop-up odds, high speed simulation to test strategies, amazing Hand Analyzer, much more!

4. TURBO OMAHA HIGH FOR WINDOWS - $89.95 - Same features as above, but tailored for Omaha High-only. Caro says program is "an electrifying research tool...it can clearly be worth thousands of dollars to any serious player. A must for Omaha High players.

5. TURBO 7 STUD 8 OR BETTER - $89.95 - Brand new with all the features you expect from the Wilson Turbo products: the latest artificial intelligence, instant advice and exact odds, play versus 2-7 opponents, enhanced data charts that can be exported or printed, the ability to fold out of turn and immediately go to the next hand, ability to peek at opponents hand, optional warning mode that warns you if a play disagrees with the advisor, and automatic testing mode that can run up to 50 tests unattended. Challenge tough computer players who vary their styles for a truly great poker game.

6. TOURNAMENT TEXAS HOLD'EM - $59.95
Set-up for tournament practice and play, this realistic simulation pits you against celebrity look-alikes. Tons of options let you control tournament size with 10 to 300 entrants, select limits, ante, rake, blind structures, freezeouts, number of rebuys and competition level of opponents - average, tough, or toughest. Pop-up status report shows how you're doing vs. the competition. Save tournaments in progress to play again later. Additional feature allows you to quickly finish a folded hand and go on to the next.